THE ZERO TAX STRATEGY

JEREMY LEDERER

FOREWORD BY MARK J. KOHLER

THE Short Book Formula PUBLISHING

Published by
The Short Book Formula Publishing

DISCLAIMER:

This book contains the opinions and ideas of the author. Careful attention has been paid to ensure the accuracy of the information, but the author cannot assume responsibility for the validity or consequences of its use. The material in this book is for informational purposes only. As each individual situation is unique, the author disclaims responsibility for any adverse effects that may result from the use or application of the information contained in this book. Any use of the information found in this book is the sole responsibility of the reader.

Table Of Contents

Foreword
By Mark J. Kohler

Over the last twenty-five years, I've watched countless business owners overpay in taxes for one simple reason: nobody ever taught them how the system actually works. They're busy building companies, creating jobs, taking risks, and reinvesting back into their businesses, yet most still approach taxes reactively instead of strategically. That's why I appreciate Jeremy Lederer and the work behind The Zero Tax Strategy.

It's clear that Jeremy genuinely cares about helping entrepreneurs the right way. He understands something that so many advisors completely overlook: potential tax savings and actual tax savings are not the same thing. Anybody can hype up giant deductions online or promise "zero tax," but real tax planning requires discipline, documentation, process, and responsibility. The difference between a smart strategy and a dangerous one usually comes down to whether the advisor and taxpayer are willing to do the work necessary to actually support it.

That matters, because entrepreneurs deserve better than confusion, fear, and reactive compliance. They deserve education and strategies that help them build long-term wealth responsibly and intentionally. Jeremy approaches this profession as both an entrepreneur and an advisor. That combination is rare. Most advisors have never actually built a business themselves, and many entrepreneurs never slow down long enough to truly understand strategy, structure, and planning.

As you read, don't look for magic tricks or easy buttons. Look for opportunities to become a more intentional business owner, because when entrepreneurs understand the rules and apply them correctly, the results can genuinely change lives. I've always believed that when money stays in the hands of responsible entrepreneurs, incredible things happen. They reinvest it into businesses, employees, families, local communities, and future opportunities. That ripple effect matters more than most people realize.

This book will challenge people to ask better

questions, think proactively, and build with a bigger vision for what's possible.

Mark J. Kohler

Introduction

Let me start by taking you to a moment that changed everything for me: It's a perfect morning at Olympic Club, the kind where the sunlight paints long shadows across that pristine green fairway. I'm lining up my shot, feeling the familiar weight of my club, when I overhear something that stops me in my tracks.

Two successful business owners – you know the type, sharp suits, confident handshakes – are having this conversation I've heard a hundred times before. One of them, looking absolutely defeated, is talking about watching half his income vanish to taxes.

"It is what it is," his friend says, with that resigned shrug we've all seen. "That's just the cost of success."

Now, let me tell you why that hits home so hard for me. You see, I learned something about taxes from my father that most people never figure out. Something that completely changes the game.

I grew up watching my dad build his business from scratch. We're talking impossible hours, huge risks, creating jobs – the whole entrepreneurial journey. But one image that's burned into my memory is Dad at our kitchen table, late at night, surrounded by tax returns while trying to solve an impossible puzzle. He was trying to solve how to grow his business while dealing with an ever-growing tax burden.

Have you ever watched someone you love face that kind of struggle? That scene at our kitchen table? It lit a fire in me. It's why I eventually made a pretty surprising career switch by trading in my golf clubs for tax code. And let me tell you, what I discovered in those volumes would change not just my life but the financial future of countless entrepreneurs and professionals across America.

The U.S. tax code is huge, but most of those pages describe ways to legally avoid taxes. And I mean avoid, not evade them. Not only that, but you could eliminate them by aligning your activities with what the government wants to encourage.

If you're holding this book, you're probably going through the same problem as those business owners I mentioned earlier. You've achieved significant success. Built a thriving business. Generated serious wealth. But something's not adding up.

You've written enough checks to the IRS to make your stomach turn. You're doing everything "right," yet you're still watching nearly half your income vanish.

If this resonates with you, you're not alone. I work with people like you every day:

- Executives earning seven figures who feel trapped by their W-2 income
- Business owners watching profits disappear to quarterly tax payments
- Real estate investors struggling to make passive losses count
- Professionals tired of being told high taxes are "just part of success."

You know there must be a better way. You've heard about others eliminating their tax burden legally. But when you've tried to explore advanced strategies, you've hit walls:

- CPAs who dismiss sophisticated approaches as "too aggressive."
- Advisors who can explain concepts and strategies but cannot implement them
- Fear about audit risk and documentation requiremcnts
- Confusion about how to execute complex strategies properly

I wrote this book to help you understand that eliminating taxes is both possible and legal. Through the right strategy, with the right team and proper implementation, you can not only save on taxes but completely eliminate them.

You'll learn not just what to do but how to do it correctly. How to document everything properly. How to sleep well at night knowing your strategies are efficient. How to transform your tax burden into wealth-building opportunities.

My real passion behind this book is to empower American entrepreneurs. You are the world's best allocators of capital. I've seen firsthand what happens when you keep those dollars instead of sending them to the government. You reinvest them into growing your business, creating jobs in your community, supporting causes you care about, and building something meaningful that lasts. When I see the extent of government waste and inefficiency, I'm even more convinced that you, the risk-takers and job creators, will put those resources to better use.

This is more than just finding loopholes or taking shortcuts. It involves understanding how the tax code really works and using it exactly as intended, which is to reward certain behaviors with tax savings.

By the end of this book, you'll understand how to:

- Legally eliminate your federal tax burden

- Create audit-proof documentation for everything you do
- Build wealth faster by reinvesting tax savings
- Create a lasting legacy for generations
- Sleep well knowing you're fully compliant

So, if you're ready to stop accepting massive tax bills as "normal" and start building real wealth, keep reading. Your mindset is about to change.

Chapter 1

The True Purpose of the Tax Code

After years in this industry, I've sat through thousands of meetings that all tell the same story. Most successful Americans are paying way too much in taxes.

Ryan[1] came into my office one day, clutching a stack of tax returns like they were burning a hole in his hands. Here's a guy who's built an incredible software company from the ground up, pulling in $1.2 million per year in profits, and he looks absolutely frustrated.

As soon as he sees me, the first thing he says is something I've heard hundreds of times: "I'm doing every-

1 Ryan is a fictional character. His story was inspired by the many clients I've worked with, who faced similar challenges.

thing my CPA told me to do, but I'm still writing these massive checks to the IRS every quarter." I could feel his frustration as he continued, "Almost half my income is going to taxes. This can't be right."

Now, here's something most people, even some CPAs, don't understand: The tax code isn't what they think it is.

See, everyone's been told the tax code is this complex system designed to take as much of your money as possible. But after spending years studying this, I mean really studying it, I can tell you that's wrong. Completely wrong.

"What would you say if I told you we could legally eliminate your federal tax burden?" I ask. Ryan looks skeptical. They all do at first. But he's interested.

Working together over the next year, we did exactly that. We eliminated his federal tax burden while staying fully compliant with every IRS rule.

But we did more than just save him money. Ryan gained the confidence that comes from understanding how the tax code really works.

I see hundreds of business owners and high-income earners pay way too much in taxes because they don't understand the one simple truth that the tax code isn't designed to take your money. It's designed to reward certain behaviors with tax savings.

Ryan's story could be yours. But first, you need to understand what the tax code is really for, and why most people, including many tax professionals, get it completely wrong. That misunderstanding is costing them millions in unnecessary taxes over their lifetime.

In this chapter, we'll discuss the true purpose of the tax code and why it holds the key to legally eliminating your tax burden. You'll discover why most people, including many tax professionals, misunderstand what the tax code is designed to do and how this misunderstanding costs them millions in unnecessary taxes over their lifetime.

The Million-Page Mystery

Everyone knows that the tax code is complex, right? But let me ask you a question. How many pages do you think there are in the tax code? The answer would probably be, "I don't know. Tons of pages?"

Well, you're not wrong. The U.S. tax code, including all related regulations and guidance, spans over a million pages.

What's even more surprising is that 99.99% of those pages describe ways to avoid or eliminate taxes.

Let that sink in for a moment.

But why would the government create such an extensive system of tax avoidance? The answer will transform how you'll think about taxes forever.

Flipping the Script: Understanding Tax Code as an Incentive System

The government knows they're not great at directly solving economic challenges like creating jobs, developing housing, or driving innovation.

But something the government is actually good at is incentivizing entrepreneurs and investors to solve these problems. This is where the tax code comes into play.

Look at Ryan's situation. His software company was already investing heavily in research and development, which is exactly the kind of activity the government wants to encourage. By properly documenting these activities and structuring his business correctly, we helped him claim substantial R&D tax credits that were sitting there waiting to be used.

We're not pushing boundaries here. These incentives are written directly into the tax code. It's like the government was literally telling you, "Do these specific things, in these specific ways, and you don't have to pay so much in taxes".

Following the Money: How Incentives Shape the Economy

So, we've just discovered that the tax code is one of the world's most elaborate incentive programs.

Now let's see how this looks in practice:

Real Estate Development

- Accelerated depreciation lets you write off property costs faster
- 1031 exchanges allow you to defer tax indefinitely on sales
- Opportunity Zone investments can eliminate capital gains entirely
- Cost segregation studies create immediate write-offs that may cover the downpayment on your investment

Energy Sector

- Solar and wind credits reward clean energy investment
- Oil and gas incentives encourage domestic energy production
- Energy-efficient building deductions promote sustainability
- Alternative fuel credits drive innovation

Job Creation and Innovation

- R&D credits reward technological advancement

- Work Opportunity Credits encourage diverse hiring
- Employee retention incentives promote stable employment
- Workforce development investments create valuable opportunities for tax deductions

Each represents an area where the government would rather reward private sector solutions than create government programs.

The Power of Proper Implementation

Understanding these incentives is just the starting point. Even sophisticated business owners like Ryan often overpay because they miss the implementation piece.

Judge Learned Hand, one of America's most respected judges, once said, "No taxpayer is required to pay more than the minimum amount due."

What he said means basically what I've been showing my clients for years. You have every right to arrange your financial affairs to pay the lowest amount of tax legally possible. The courts haven't just suggested this. They've consistently defended it as a fundamental right of every taxpayer.

But the key is that these strategies must be implemented correctly with proper documentation and compliance to be effective.

The Regulatory Reality: Understanding How It Works

Most people think Congress just passes tax laws, and that's it. But most of the opportunities I use to help clients eliminate taxes don't come from Congress at all.

When was the last time you saw Congress, the Senate, and the President all agree on a major tax bill? It rarely happens. It happens maybe once every decade or so. But tax rules and opportunities change all the time. How? Regulatory guidance.

Here's what I mean. Instead of waiting for Congress to pass new laws, the IRS and Treasury Department regularly issue what we call "guidance," which are detailed instructions about how to use different parts of the tax code. These are powerful tools that tell us exactly how to qualify for tax benefits.

This is where most people miss out. They focus on the big tax laws but ignore all this regulatory guidance. It's like having a treasure map but missing all the detailed instructions that tell you exactly where to dig.

Once you understand how these regulations work, they become your blueprint for success. Every regulation comes with specific steps for qualification. Follow these steps exactly, document everything properly, and you've built an iron-clad position for eliminating taxes completely legally.

Historical Proof: A Legacy of Success

The U.S. tax code's power to shape America's economy is written in our history.

Let me share some examples:

1. **The mortgage interest deduction (1913)** - the government wanted to turn America into a nation of homeowners. Instead of launching a massive federal housing program, they created something simpler. The mortgage interest deduction. This single change in the tax code sparked the largest middle-class wealth-building opportunity we've ever seen.
2. **World War II Industrial Mobilization (1940s)** - America needed to rapidly transform its industrial capacity. Rather than having the government build factories, the tax code incentivized private companies to expand. The result was that American industry exploded with growth, creating an economic powerhouse that dominated the post-war world. Private businesses, guided by smart tax incentives, accomplished what no government program could have done alone.

3. **Energy Tax Credits (1970s to present)** - Back in 1978, America faced an energy crisis. The solution wasn't for the government to build solar panels or wind farms. Instead, they created energy investment tax credits. These incentives sparked an entire renewable energy industry that continues growing today. What started as a tax incentive has turned into thousands of new businesses, countless jobs, and technological innovations that are transforming our energy future.

Each example shows that the government identifies a need and creates tax incentives. Then private enterprise does what it does best. It innovates, grows, and creates wealth in the process.

This is the same playbook you can use today. The tax code is still full of these opportunities. They're just waiting for you to find that professional who understands how to use them.

Modern Opportunities

Today's tax code offers even more sophisticated opportunities than these historical examples.

Take the 2017 Opportunity Zone legislation, for example. It allows investors to defer, reduce, and potentially eliminate capital gains taxes while investing in designated development areas.

This single program demonstrates how modern tax incentives can simultaneously:

- Eliminate taxes for investors
- Drive economic development
- Create jobs in underserved areas
- Generate long-term wealth
- Align private profit with public good

Your Path Forward

Understanding the tax code's true purpose helps, but it's not enough. The real magic happens in implementation.

1. **Identify Relevant Incentives** - This is often the most exciting part for my clients. They discover that their existing business activities could qualify for substantial tax benefits they never knew existed. Just like Ryan and his software company, you might be sitting on tax-saving opportunities hidden in plain sight.

2. **Create Proper Documentation** - This is crucial. I've seen too many entrepreneurs try to claim tax benefits without proper support, only to face problems later. Make sure to include clear records of your activities and decisions, properly organized

financial documentation, and evidence that supports your tax positions.

3. **Structure Operations Correctly** - This might mean setting up the right types of business entities and timing your activities to align with tax years to ensure that all your strategies work together.

4. **Monitor and Adjust** - The tax code evolves, and your strategy needs to evolve with it. Forget about checking boxes once a year. You need to build a dynamic approach that grows with your business.

I've seen clients transform their financial future by following these steps. Be cautioned that this isn't a do-it-yourself project.

Just like you wouldn't build a house without an architect and contractor, you shouldn't implement tax strategies without expert guidance. The potential savings are too significant to risk getting it wrong.

Conclusion

Let's return to Ryan. Once he understood the tax code's true purpose and implemented the right strategies, everything changed. Instead of sending nearly half his income to the IRS, he redirected those funds into growing his business, creating jobs, and building wealth.

You're facing the same choice Ryan did. You can continue viewing the tax code as a burden designed to extract maximum taxes, or you can recognize it for what it really is: a sophisticated system of incentives designed to reward specific behaviors with tax elimination.

But the difference is working with the right professional and focusing on implementation.

In the next chapter, we'll explore the Four Circles of Wealth Creation, or the framework that turns this understanding into reality. You'll learn exactly how to implement these strategies in your own situation, creating the same transformative results Ryan and countless others have achieved.

Chapter 2

The Four Converging Circles of Wealth Creation

One of my favorite moments in this business is when I get to show clients something that completely changes how they think about taxes. Let me take you to one of those moments.

I'm walking through Tom's[2] Craft Distillery, and let me tell you, this place is something special. The moment you step inside, that sweet, oaky scent of aging whiskey hits you. You've got these beautiful copper stills gleaming against the walls, rows of charred oak barrels stretching as far as you can see, and, right outside, there's

2. Tom is a fictional character. His story is based on the many clients I've worked with who faced similar challenges.

this impressive new 30,000 square foot building that's about to double their production.

Tom, a long-time client, has built something special here. His whiskey wins awards, and demand keeps growing. But there's tension in his voice as he shows me around. A few days later, sitting in my office, he finally explains why.

"I thought expanding was the right move," he says, running his hands through his hair in frustration.

"The business is growing like crazy. But between this $3 million building purchase and our regular tax bill, we're getting squeezed." He pauses, shaking his head. "My CPA says we can only deduct about 2.5% of the building cost each year. At this rate, it'll take 39 years to write it off!"

I've heard this story hundreds of times. Successful business owners usually get caught in this brutal cycle. The more their business grows, the more taxes eat into the capital they need for expansion.

Their CPAs follow standard practices, treating buildings like single assets depreciated over decades. It's textbook accounting, but it's costing people like Tom hundreds of thousands in unnecessary taxes.

"So you're telling me I'm stuck making tiny deductions for the next four decades while paying massive tax bills now?" Tom asks, his voice rising with disbelief. "That can't be right."

What Tom was missing is that tax strategy means building a comprehensive approach that works together.

That day, Tom understood what I call the Four Circles of Wealth Creation. Implementing these strategies completely transformed his life.

Because Tom used the facility exclusively for his business, we were able to aggregate the real estate activity with the business activity. This critical step made it possible to implement a cost segregation study, which is a strategy that identifies portions of a building that can be depreciated much faster than the standard 39-year timeline.

The results were dramatic. Instead of tiny deductions spread over nearly four decades, Tom received about $275,000 in tax savings the first year alone, all completely legal and by the book.

Instead of writing massive checks to the IRS, Tom reinvested those savings directly back into his business, in ways like adding more whiskey barrels, expanding his staff, and purchasing new distillery equipment. The result was that his business doubled in size the very next year.

The next time I visit the distillery, there's a completely different energy in the air. Tom's not just proud of his whiskey anymore. He's also confident about his business's future.

"I wish I'd known about this years ago," Tom tells me as we watch his team fill another barrel. "Now I understand that it's all about building a complete system."

That's the real transformation I want to share with you. Gaining this confidence comes from understanding how these four circles work together to create lasting results.

In this chapter, I'll walk you through these Four Circles of Wealth Creation in detail. You'll discover how Tax Efficiency, Leverage, Velocity, and Specialization work together as a complete system, why implementing them correctly is crucial, and how they can transform your financial future, just like they did for Tom.

The Power of a Complete System

Most tax strategies fail because they focus on individual tactics instead of building a comprehensive system. It's like looking at a single piece of a puzzle without seeing the whole picture.

The Four Circles work together as a complete system, and each one makes the others more powerful as they converge on your dream:

- **Tax Efficiency** is your foundation. Most people think it's all about finding deductions, but there's so much more to it than that. I'll detail six specific elements that allow the tax code to work in your favor later.

- **Specialization** means focusing on what works best for your specific situation. You don't need to know everything about taxes. You just need to master the strategies that matter most to you.
- **Velocity** is all about timing. When you implement a strategy can be just as important as which strategy you choose. I've seen clients miss out on hundreds of thousands in savings just by waiting a few weeks too long.
- **Leverage** is where things get interesting. This is how we multiply your results. One strategy might save you money, but when you combine strategies the right way? That's when the magic happens.

See Graphic on Next Page

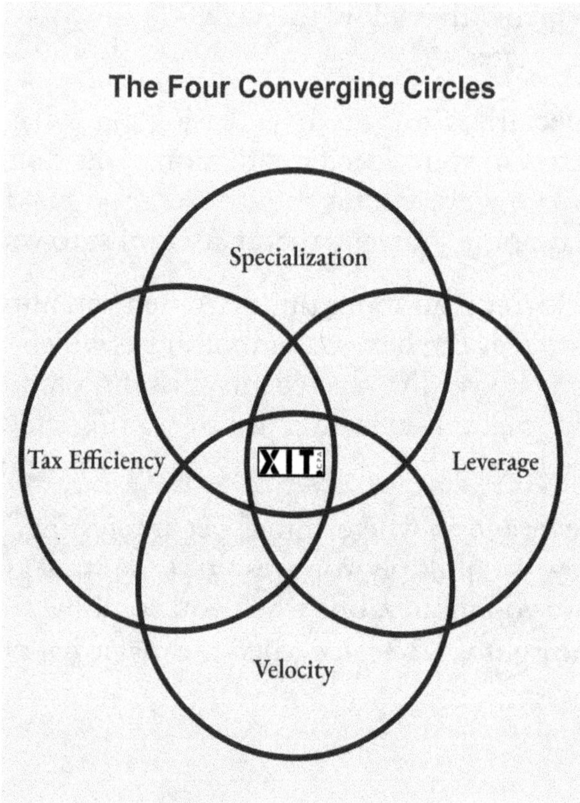

Each circle is important on its own, but together they create something stable and strong. At the center is your financial goal. My team and I at XIT CPA are dedicated to helping you meet these goals.

Let's examine each in detail and see how they create transformative results when properly implemented.

Circle 1: Tax Efficiency
The Foundation

Tax efficiency is like having a good map. Without it, you might eventually reach your destination, but you'll waste time and money getting there.

Let me show you the six elements that make this work:

1. **Entity Structuring:** This means choosing the right tool for the job. Setting up the right type of business (like LLCs or partnerships) creates the foundation for everything else. The focus is on building structures that work together with clear separation between activities.

2. **Strategic Deductions:** Sure, we'll claim all your eligible write-offs, but we need to look deeper than the obvious ones. Anything that's ordinary, necessary, and reasonable in pursuing income is deductible. With proper documentation, even areas many consider "gray" like travel, meals, or home office expenses become legitimate deductions.

3. **Income Conversion:** Some types of income get taxed more heavily than others. The trick is knowing how to transform highly-taxed income into more tax-friendly categories. This might involve material participation strategies or even something as simple as an S-Corp election to

convert self-employment income into more tax-efficient business income.

4. **Bracket Optimization:** Taxation is progressive. Everyone benefits from lower tax brackets before moving to higher rates. Not all bracket jumps are equal, with significant leaps like the one from 24% to 32%. When you have to pay some taxes, optimize which brackets that income falls into.
5. **Elimination Strategies:** Yes, permanently eliminating taxes is possible, and it's completely legal. With intentional planning, you can do it with tax credits, opportunity zones, and properly structured real estate investments.
6. **Strategic Tax Deferral:** Remember, when you act matters as much as what you do. Delaying taxes with strategies like retirement accounts, installment sales, or property exchanges gives you control over when you pay them, creating significant advantages.

Circle 2: Specialization - Mastering Your Strategy

You don't need to know everything about taxes. You just need to master what matters most for your situation. That's exactly how we approach tax strategy.

Successful specialization comes from three important areas that work together to create lasting results.

1. **Choose the Right Focus:** This means understanding what strategies align naturally with your business and goals. You should focus on something you already know about, or are genuinely interested in. When you're passionate about something, you'll naturally learn more about it, which reduces risk. The more you understand a strategy, the less intimidating it becomes, and the more confident you'll be in implementing it properly.

2. **Build Deep Knowledge:** Don't get me wrong. I'm not saying you should become a tax expert yourself, but you should understand enough to make informed decisions, especially when recourse debt is involved. Tax laws change constantly, and what worked last year might not work this year. It's important to learn and adapt.

3. **Maintain Expert Support:** You need the right support team. Even Olympic athletes need a good coach to get to the podium, and this is no different. Work with professionals who have walked this path before. They should bring both expertise and experience with situations like yours.

Circle 3: Velocity - The Power of Speed

When we talk about velocity, we're not thinking about rushing. We mean executing strategies at the right time to maximize their impact.

Here's why velocity matters:

1. **Tax Deadlines Are Absolute:** The clock is always ticking. Miss the December 31 deadline for implementing a strategy, and you might wait a full year to see the benefits.
2. **Market Opportunities Don't Wait:** Opportunities don't wait. You have just 180 days to reinvest capital gains into an Opportunity Zone to defer taxes. By moving quickly and having the right team in place, you can execute the strategy with weeks to spare.
3. **Documentation Must Keep Pace:** Fast implementation requires equally fast documentation. I can't tell you how many times I've seen good strategies fail because the paperwork lagged behind.

Circle 4: Leverage - Multiplying Your Impact

Our second circle is leverage. Leverage makes those tax strategies work together to multiply your results.

Important aspects of leverage:

1. **Recourse vs. Non-recourse Debt:** recourse debt is when you're personally guaranteeing the loan. That means if things go south, the lender can come after more than just the property or asset you borrowed against. Non-recourse debt works differently. This puts a fence around the asset you're borrowing against. If something goes wrong, the lender can only take what's inside that fence. They can't touch your other assets. Although recourse debt may have more risk to some, it may yield significantly higher after-tax return on investment (ROI).

2. **Team Collaboration:** No single person can master every aspect of tax strategy. That's why we build teams of specialists with CPAs, attorneys, and other experts who work together to implement complex strategies correctly.

3. **Strategic Leverage:** This takes all the individual pieces and makes them work together to multiply your results. For example, combining cost segregation with recourse debt and material participation can multiply your tax savings while building long-term wealth.

Leverage can help you maximize your tax savings while expanding your wealth. The right team and an understanding of financial tools will work together to amplify your results while managing risks.

Making the Circles Work Together

The real power comes when all four circles work in concert. At Tom's distillery:

- **Tax Efficiency:** We identified the optimal depreciation strategy for his new building.
- **Specialization:** We focused specifically on strategies relevant to real estate and manufacturing.
- **Velocity:** We implemented everything before year-end to secure immediate benefits.
- **Leverage:** We used proper debt structuring to maximize available deductions.

The result is where the four circles converge and the most efficient way for Tom to achieve his wealth dream.

Conclusion

Whether you're a W-2 earner or a business owner, these circles work. The specific strategies might change, but the framework remains the same. As we finish the chapter, I want to suggest some action steps:

- First, review your tax situation with fresh eyes.
- Second, evaluate your team. Do they understand tax strategies? Can they implement complex situations?

- Third, pay attention to your timeline. What deadlines are approaching? How can you prepare yourself for the next year?

Just like our friend Tom, you might be sitting on some tax-saving opportunities hidden in plain sight. The key is knowing how to unlock them using all four pillars together.

In the next chapter, we'll explore why most tax strategies fail and how proper implementation makes the difference between success and failure. You'll learn exactly what documentation you need and how to protect yourself from IRS scrutiny while maximizing your tax savings.

Chapter 3

Why Most Tax Strategies Fail: The Implementation Gap

In her corner office in San Diego, Amanda was living proof that being brilliant at complex problems doesn't always translate to tax success. As the owner of a fast-growing biotech company, she had tax courses stacked on her desk, seminar notes organized perfectly. She even had YouTube tutorials carefully transcribed. But something wasn't clicking.

During our Zoom call, she leaned back in her chair, the frustration clear on her face. "I don't get it, Jeremy. In my business, I solve impossible scientific and operational problems all day. But these tax strategies?" She gestured at the stack of materials surrounding her.

"Nothing's delivering the results I expected."

What made Amanda's situation so interesting was her track record. She'd built her biotech company into a thriving enterprise with multiple patents and growing revenue. Other executives in her industry sought her advice on scaling their operations. She was that good. But implementing tax strategies for her business? That's where everything fell apart.

Her preparation was impeccable. She had detailed flowcharts, mapped-out strategies, and every concept thoroughly researched. She could explain the most intricate details of each approach. But something crucial was missing.

"Amanda," I told her, "your understanding of these strategies is spot-on. They absolutely work. But what you're missing is implementation."

The moment those words landed, I saw recognition flash across her face. She was about to discover why all her perfectly planned strategies weren't translating into actual savings.

Amanda's story resonates with so many brilliant business owners. These are people who can disrupt entire industries with innovation but miss the critical piece that turns tax strategy from an expensive hobby into real savings for their companies.

In this chapter, we're investigating why tax strategies fail, even when you understand them completely. You'll see the common implementation problems that derail even the best strategies, and more importantly, how to fix them.

The Knowledge-Action Gap

Understanding tax strategy and making it work are two completely different things. Amanda knew every detail about tax strategies. But knowing the theory isn't the same as implementing it effectively for her biotech company.

Amanda got stuck because she tried making real estate investing a tax strategy. Great idea in theory, but there was a big problem. To qualify as a real estate professional for tax purposes, you need to spend at least 750 hours annually in real estate activities, and it needs to be your primary business activity.

But when you're running a fast-growing biotech company that's demanding 60+ hours of your week, hitting those real estate hours is practically impossible. Amanda was caught in that classic trap. She had great intentions but the wrong strategy for her specific situation.

That's when we shifted her focus to healthcare software Right to Use (RTU) strategies, something that aligned perfectly with her industry expertise. The beauty of this pivot was that her biotech background made it possible to achieve material participation in the health-care software investment. This allowed us to convert what would typically be passive losses into active losses that could directly offset the income from her biotech business.

You see how powerful this is? Instead of just looking for any tax strategy, we found one that complemented her existing business knowledge and time constraints.

Amanda's example showed us that intelligence and technical knowledge aren't enough. Even the smartest entrepreneurs find difficulties putting what they know into action. This is what I call the Knowledge-Action Gap.

You need three critical pieces working together to turn tax strategies into real savings:

1. **Documentation Systems:** Stop seeing documentation as just paperwork. This is your protection. When you track activities and transactions as they happen, you're building a shield against IRS scrutiny. A rock-solid documentation should include time logs that show exactly what you did and when, meeting minutes that capture key decisions, and financial records that tell the complete story of your business activities.

2. **Team Coordination:** Your team is like the structural framework of a skyscraper. Your CPA pro-

vides strategic oversight, making sure every move aligns with your tax goals. Attorneys handle the legal structure, while financial advisors ensure your investments support your strategy. Regular communication keeps everyone moving in the same direction.

3. **Execution Timeline:** Timing matters. You need the right things happening in the right order. You start with strategy development, move through entity formation, and then implement your systems. But it doesn't stop there. Just like a house needs maintenance, your strategy needs regular monitoring to stay effective.

When these three elements work together, your strategy becomes virtually bulletproof. But if any one of these elements is weak or missing, the entire structure becomes vulnerable.

Why Smart People Make Basic Mistakes

Let me ask you a simple question. What's the difference between having a perfect recipe and creating an amazing meal?

You can understand every ingredient and technique perfectly, but until you're actually in the kitchen timing each step and coordinating every element, you just have a really good idea, not a meal.

Tax strategy works the same way. There's a world of difference between knowing what to do and making it happen.

Strategy is your roadmap. You identify opportunities, understand tax code incentives, and create plans that align with your goals. Amanda had this part down perfectly. She knew exactly which strategies could work for her situation.

But implementation is where most strategies either succeed or fall apart.

Successful implementation means coordinating with multiple professionals, hitting specific deadlines, maintaining precise documentation, and ensuring everything aligns perfectly with IRS requirements.

This explains why brilliant professionals often struggle with tax strategy. They put all their energy into understanding the what without mastering the how. They collect strategies like recipes but never learn the crucial techniques that bring them to life.

But the good news is once you understand this difference, everything changes. Because implementation isn't about working harder - it's about working smarter, with systems and processes that ensure every strategy delivers results.

Aspect	Strategy	Implementation
Focus	Planning and designing solutions	Executing and operationalizing plans
Activity	Identifying opportunities	Taking actionable steps to realize goals
Example	Deciding to use an S-Corp structure	Filing IRS Form 2553 to elect S-Corp status
Documentation	Conceptual framework	Detailed records to substantiate actions
Timing	Ongoing planning	Time-sensitive execution
Role of Experts	Advisory and planning	Operational support and compliance
Outcome	A strategic plan	Realized tax savings and benefits

Common Implementation Failures

After years in this industry, I've noticed that sometimes being smart can work against you. The same qualities that make you successful in your field can become obstacles in tax strategy implementation.

The Analysis Paralysis Trap

This hits my highly analytical clients hard. They spend months analyzing every detail. They consider valuation methods, legal requirements, and long-term implications. They might have a solid strategy with substantial tax savings potential. But by the time they feel ready to move forward, we've missed the year-end deadline.

That single delay means waiting an entire year before seeing any tax benefits. A perfect strategy becomes useless through perfect analysis.

The costs add up quickly:

- You miss deadlines for current-year tax benefits.
- Strategic timing opportunities slip away.
- Crucial structures remain unimplemented.
- You might end up rushing execution at the last minute, increasing your risk of mistakes.

Communication solves this problem. Sometimes it's sharing experiences, connecting clients with others who've been there, or simply showing the actual dollar amount they're losing by waiting. When they see the specific costs of delay, everything shifts.

Documentation: The Silent Killer

Documentation is another silent killer of tax strategies. "I'll document it later". These four words have derailed more tax strategies than any IRS audit. If you want to be successful in your tax implementation strategies, you need proper documentation.

The Proper Documentation Checklist		
For Material Participation	**For Entity Structures**	**For Private Equity Investments**
☐ Detailed time logs with specific activities	☐ Formation documents	☐ Purchase agreements
☐ Meeting minutes and agendas	☐ Operating agreements	☐ Financing documents
☐ Email correspondence related to business	☐ Bank account records	☐ Proof of payment
☐ Contracts and agreements	☐ Transaction documentation	☐ Investment purpose statements
☐ Evidence of decision-making authority	☐ Board meeting minutes	☐ Risk assessment documentation
	☐ Annual compliance filings	☐ Performance tracking records

Proper documentation is essential for the successful implementation of tax strategies. It supports your tax claims, keeps you in line with tax laws, and protects you in case of an audit.

Timing Failures

The December Rush is real. Every year, without fail, my phone starts ringing in December with people wanting to implement complex tax strategies before year-end. But what most people don't understand about timing is that some critical deadlines can't be rushed.

Real examples include:

- Entity formations and elections
- Real estate closings
- Investment funding requirements
- Documentation establishment
- Team assembly and coordination

Missing deadlines can make you miss out on time-sensitive tax savings and not be able to claim benefits later. Pay attention to that.

Incomplete Execution

Here's another problem. Partial implementation is like building half a bridge. You've spent the resources but can't get to the other side.

Imagine a real estate investor who sets up the perfect entity structure but never opens separate bank accounts. In an IRS audit, they could disregard his entire structure because he can't prove separate business operations.

I don't mean to scare you, but I do want you to pay attention to the details. Incomplete execution could make your tax benefits be denied simply because you didn't complete the process.

Poor Fact Patterns

Facts matter more than strategy. The IRS doesn't care what you intended to do. They care what you can prove you did.

Imagine that you invested in a rental property and claimed substantial losses against your W-2 income. Seems a good strategy, right? But if you don't have actual evidence on that rental activity, you could have some problems.

So, this lack of organization about your income, expenses, or investments could definitely make it harder for you to achieve the tax benefits you want.

And how do you overcome that? You must create proper fact patterns.

Here are some steps you could follow to make it easier:

Before Implementation:

- Clear business purpose documentation
- Written plans and projections
- Entity structure alignment
- Team role definitions
- Investment Due Diligence

During Operation:

- Regular activity logs
- Financial transaction records
- Meeting documentation
- Communication records
- Progress tracking

To Reduce Audit Risk:

- Third-party verifications
- Independent valuations
- Expert opinions
- Timeline documentation
- Supporting evidence

Building an Implementation System That Works

Success requires more than good systems. It needs accountability. Implementation should be automatic rather than burdensome.

Weekly actions form your foundation. Review time logs to keep them current. Document transactions as they happen, not weeks later. Track activities to maintain honest participation levels. Regular team updates ensure everyone stays aligned.

Monthly, we dig deeper. Check how your actions align with overall strategy. Scrutinize documentation to maintain audit-readiness. Review bank statements. Assess progress toward tax-saving goals. Track achievements. This monthly rhythm catches issues before they become problems.

Quarterly sessions bring your entire team together. These are comprehensive strategy reviews. We look for documentation gaps and emerging risks in the regulatory environment. We consider estimated tax payments and opportunities for improvement. This keeps your tax strategy bulletproof.

Annual planning optimizes your strategy based on the year's lessons. We evaluate team performance, update systems, set clear goals for the year ahead, and consider additional strategies to optimize your position while there's still time. Think of it as your tax strategy's annual checkup - ensuring everything's ready for another year of tax savings.

This framework builds habits that make tax savings automatic rather than stressful. When you follow this rhythm, implementation becomes second nature.

Conclusion

Implementation transforms good ideas into actual tax savings. Think about Amanda. She had all the knowledge but couldn't turn it into results until she built the right systems.

Once we shifted to the healthcare software RTU strategy that aligned with her biotech expertise and implemented it properly, the results spoke for themselves. With just a $100,000 investment, Amanda purchased $700,000 worth of software units that qualified for both Section 168 and Section 179 depreciation. By optimizing these tax code provisions, we created a $700,000 deduction in year one that directly offset income from her biotech company.

Since Amanda's business is in California, with combined federal and state tax rates approaching 50%, that $700,000 deduction translated to approximately $350,000 in actual tax savings. A $100,000 investment generated $350,000 in real tax savings. These were not deferred taxes or minor reductions. They were actual dollars that stayed in her business instead of going to the government.

Proper implementation turns tax strategy from an expensive hobby into a powerful wealth-building tool.

In the next chapter, we'll explore how to convert these tax savings into wealth-building opportunities. You'll learn exactly how to reinvest your savings for maximum growth while maintaining the audit protection we've discussed here.

Chapter 4

Converting Tax Payments into Wealth-Building Opportunities

I remember sitting in a busy coffee shop with Mark[3], one of those rare executives who seemed to have mastered the corporate game.

He has seven-figure business profits and a high W-2 , thriving investment portfolio, and a collection of rental properties. He checked every box of traditional success. Most people looking at Mark's life would think, *"Now there's someone who's got it all figured out."*

This wasn't meant to be a business meeting. It was just two colleagues catching up. But that morning, watch-

3 Mark is a fictional character. His story is based on the many clients I've worked with who faced similar challenges.

ing him stir his packet of sugar into his coffee, I could see something weighing heavily on his mind. Then he brought up his taxes, and everything shifted.

"You know what kills me?" he asked, pulling out his phone to show me his financial dashboard. "Every year, I watch so much money disappear. $400,000 to federal, another $100,000 to state. A decade of making seven figures, and my net worth has barely moved in the last three years."

I couldn't help but smile. Not because of Mark's frustration but because I'd heard this story countless times before. Here was someone doing everything by the conventional playbook yet missing the opportunities hiding in plain sight.

Over the next year, working together, we didn't just save Mark money. We fundamentally transformed his approach to wealth building. That $400,000 that used to vanish into the federal coffers became the foundation of a sophisticated investment portfolio generating additional annual income on top of his executive salary.

The real transformation, though, wasn't in the numbers. It was in Mark's understanding of something most professionals never grasp. The tax code isn't a system designed to take your money. It's a roadmap showing you how to keep it...if you know how to read the signs.

In this chapter, we'll explore how to convert tax payments into wealth-building opportunities. More importantly, you'll discover how to implement these strategies in your own situation, step by step.

The Wealth-Building Mindset Shift

When it comes to transforming tax payments into wealth, the first step is shifting how you think about taxes and overcoming the natural hesitation that comes with advanced tax strategies.

After spending years in this field, I've noticed a pattern. Even the most successful business owners often stick to basic tax strategies, simply accepting taxes as an inevitable burden.

But there's something deeper at play. They have a fear of implementing more sophisticated approaches, worried about potential IRS scrutiny or making costly mistakes.

Trust me, I understand this hesitation completely. When clients first hear about advanced tax strategies, their initial reaction is usually skepticism. "Isn't this pushing the envelope too far?" they ask. "What happens if we get audited?"

Avoiding advanced tax strategies because you're worried about IRS scrutiny is like refusing to fix a leaking boat because you're afraid of making the hole bigger.

The reality is that these strategies aren't aggressive at all. They're precisely what the tax code was designed to encourage.

This is exactly why education forms the foundation of everything we do. Before implementing any strategy, we break down not just what we're doing but also why it works and how it aligns perfectly with tax law.

Through comprehensive documentation and step-by-step explanations, our clients discover that these strategies are simply following the tax code exactly as intended.

Real transformation begins when this fundamental truth clicks. Every dollar paid in taxes represents potential investment capital that could be working for you instead of being given to the government. But using this capital effectively isn't about taking risks. It's about following a proven, well-documented process.

From Complex to Clear

One lesson stands out from years of implementing these strategies. Complexity kills execution.

That's why we break down every strategy into clear, actionable steps. We start with the immediate pain point, showing exactly what you're currently paying in taxes, those hundreds of thousands vanishing each year.

From there, we demonstrate how specific strategies can transform that tax burden into wealth-building opportunities. But theory isn't enough. We map out precise implementation steps, covering:

- Required entity formations
- Investment structuring guidelines
- Documentation requirements
- Risk mitigation protocols

Each step aligns perfectly with government incentives while ensuring complete protection.

When you see how these pieces fit together, complexity fades away. What seemed risky becomes secure, backed by solid documentation and proven processes.

Strategic Reinvestment Pathways

Once you've shifted your mindset about taxes, the next step is understanding where to redirect those tax savings.

This doesn't mean throwing money into random investments hoping something sticks. Before recommending any strategy, we dive deep into the analysis, ensuring it's not just legally sound but also perfectly suited to your specific situation.

These are carefully designed routes that multiply your wealth while preserving the tax benefits that freed up your capital in the first place.

This is where velocity, one of the Four Circles we discussed in Chapter 2, becomes crucial.

Simply saving on taxes isn't enough. Precise documentation and proper protection help to redirect those savings quickly into investments that generate return. The faster you move with the right safeguards in place, the more powerful the compounding effect becomes.

Breaking Down Advanced Strategies

Something crucial to understand is that whether you're earning a W-2 salary or running your own business, reaching zero taxes involves leveraging advanced strategies that most tax professionals never discuss.

There are four powerful approaches that can transform your tax situation:

Charitable Holding Company Strategy

Imagine having your own private foundation but with enhanced control and superior tax benefits. A Charitable Holding Company allows you to:

- Make tax-deductible contributions of cash or appreciated assets

- Maintain full control over investment and distribution decisions
- Create immediate tax deductions while building lasting legacy
- Only pay 1% of capital gains tax when assets are sold
- Avoid 100% of estate taxes to maximize legacy
- Fund worthy charities in the most tax efficient way possible

Here's a real example:

Imagine you're about to sell an asset worth $5 million. This could be anything from real estate to a business to paper assets (like stocks and crypto) to commodities (like gold and Bitcoin). Any asset class works here (unlike the more limited 1031 exchange for real estate).

Instead of selling directly and facing substantial capital gains taxes, you gift the asset to your Charitable Holding Company. This creates an immediate charitable deduction that could potentially offset up to 50% of your taxable income for the year.

When the Charitable Holding Company sells that asset, you avoid 99% of the capital gains tax. That's right. You're only paying 1% tax on that gain because of the intentional way we've structured the entity.

Now your Charitable Holding Company has significant capital to work with. From there, the possibilities multiply. We coordinate with attorneys to ensure everything is properly structured, but this strategy creates incredible flexibility for both tax savings and charitable impact.

Liquidation Event
December 2024

Proposed (Charitable Holding Company) Structure

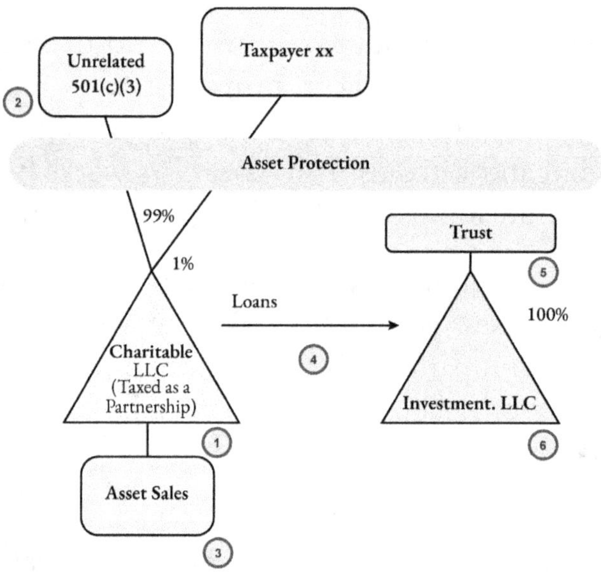

Footnotes

1 Charitable LLC setup and appreciated asset contributed before liquidation event. This generates a non-cash charitable deduction.

2 Operating agreement specifies that nonprofit has no voting rights and manager of LLC retains 100% control with only 1% ownership interest. Nonprofit is entitled benefits as majority owner that include annual cash distributions.

3 99% of capital gains are attributed to tax-exempt 501(c)(3) when the asset is sold. Manager of LLC is responsible for investing the proceeds.

4 Manager may decide to loan the proceeds at arms length and aligned with IRS approved interest rates to an investment LLC. The is collateralized by life insurance.

Irrevocable trust may be setup outside the taxpayer's estate to mitigate estate taxes and improve assetprotection. Taxpayer may be both trustee and beneficiary, and preserve the wealth generated for future generations.

5 Irrevocable trust may be setup outside the taxpayer's estate to mitigate estate taxes and improve asset protection. Taxpayer may be both trustee and beneficiary, and preserve the wealth generated for future generations.

6 Investment LLC may invest in anything its manager desires. It may have subsidiaries. It will eventually pay the Charitable LLC back with cheaper dollars that compounded faster due to tax efficiency of capital gains tax avoidance.

Healthcare Software RTU (Right to Use)

This strategy packs a powerful punch because it combines substantial tax benefits with potential income generation. It can:

- Generate significant upfront tax deductions through a leveraged purchase of software units and depreciation
- Create ongoing income streams through licensing revenue
- Benefit from software development incentives built into the tax code
- Receive a multiple of your initial investment in future liquidity event
- Support healthcare and technological innovation while reducing your tax burden

Remember Amanda, our brilliant biotech executive from the last chapter? This is the exact strategy aligned perfectly with her industry expertise and time constraints.

The numbers work because this is a leveraged investment using recourse debt (meaning you're potentially responsible for more than just your initial investment). While this creates more risk, it significantly increases rewards when properly implemented.

For every $100,000 you invest, you're acquiring about $700,000 worth of software. The company finances the additional $600,000, but you get a deduction for the entire $700,000 through Section 179 accelerated depreciation.

Let's break down the ROI. If you're in the highest federal tax bracket (37%), that $700,000 deduction translates to approximately $259,000 in federal tax savings alone. That's a 259% return just on the federal tax benefits, and we haven't even factored in state tax savings yet!

But it gets better. This is also a private equity investment. The founders typically plan to sell the company in the future, potentially returning not just your initial capital but a multiple of it based on the deal size.

When that liquidating event occurs, we have additional strategies to minimize taxes on those gains. Tax laws will likely change by then, but we continuously adapt our approach to maximize your benefits under whatever rules are in place.

Film Financing

Most people don't realize the entertainment industry offers unique tax advantages worth considering:

- Get immediate write-offs for qualified film investments
- Participate in profits from successful projects

- Leverage deductions to multiply your tax savings
- Support American film production while reducing your tax burden

This strategy is particularly attractive because film financing is another leveraged investment, typically structured with a four-to-one ratio. For every $100,000 you invest, you generate a $400,000 tax deduction.

One thing I love about this strategy is how accessible it makes the material participation requirement. If you're investing in films with actors or directors whose work you enjoy, time spent watching their previous films can actually count toward your 100 hours of material participation. Yes, you read that correctly! Your research (watching movies) can help qualify you for these substantial tax benefits!

At the highest federal tax bracket (37%), a $400,000 deduction creates approximately $148,000 in tax savings. That's an immediate 148% return on your $100,000 investment through tax benefits alone, not counting any potential profits from the film's success.

Leveraged Equipment Rental

Think of this as combining multiple tax benefits into one powerful package:

- Capture depreciation benefits from equipment ownership

- Generate steady income through rental payments
- Deduct interest from financing
- Write off business expenses

The leveraged equipment rental strategy typically offers a six-to-one ratio. For every $100,000 you invest, you're generating a $600,000 investment in equipment.

This strategy works particularly well if you already have a business with equipment needs. We put the equipment into service, generate rental income, and fully depreciate the equipment under Section 179 (assuming we establish the proper fact pattern).

Passive Income Generator (PIG)

This is one of my signature strategies, and it's perfect if you have elderly parents or young children. We create a management company that's partially owned by your children or parents. Your main business contracts with this management company, creating passive income for them. At the same time, they also own interests in your real estate investments, which generate passive losses. The result is the passive income and losses net to zero on their returns, while creating substantial tax benefits for your family as a whole.

See Graphics on the Following Pages

**Business Owner
December 2025**

Proposed (PIG/PAL) Structure

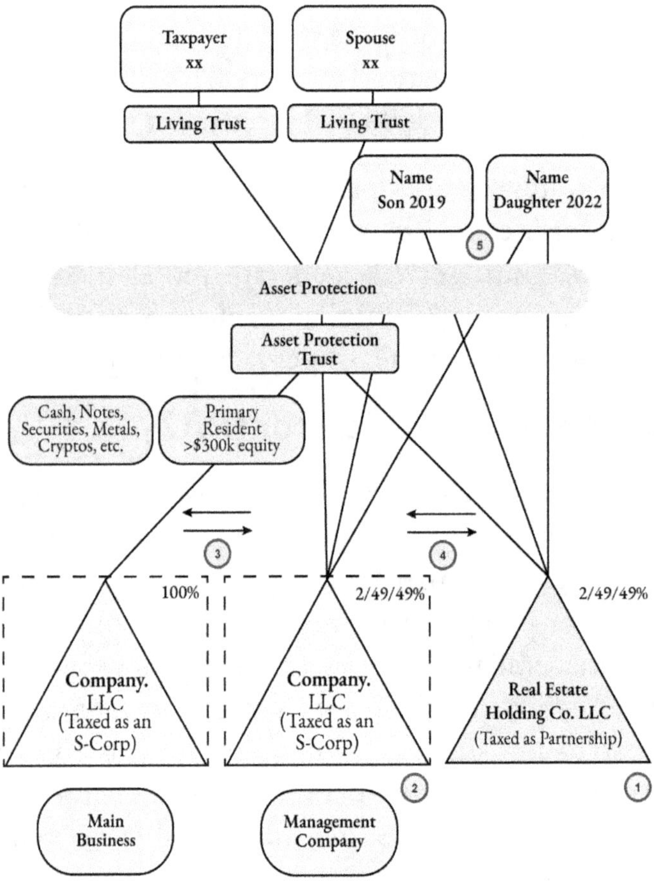

Part 2 on the following page →

Part 2 "Business Owner"

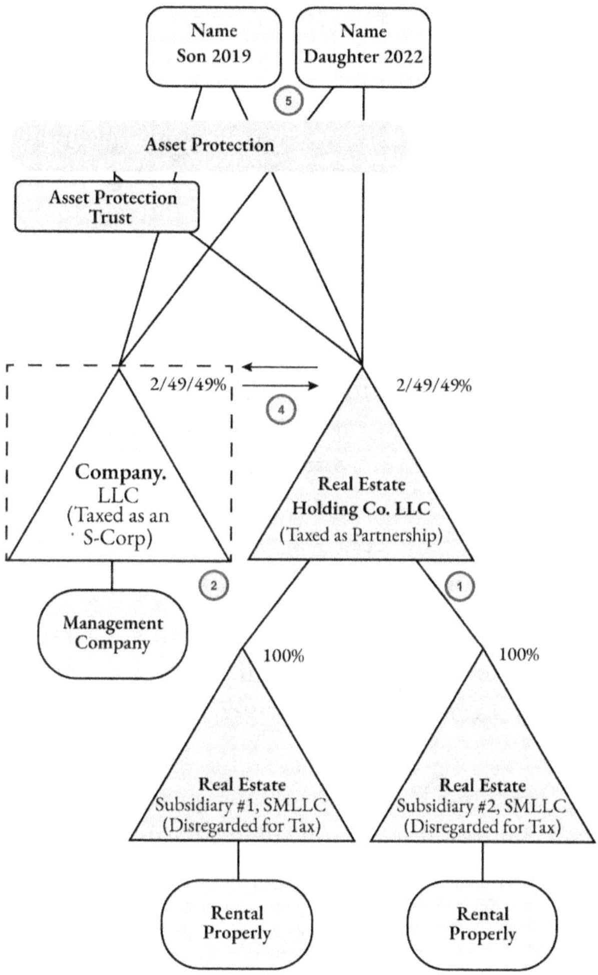

Footnotes

1 Real Estate holding company setup for long-term rental real estate investors that cannot qualify as Real Estate Professionals (REP) for tax purposes. Passive activity losses (PAL) are passed through to owners via K-1. 100% voting rights and control may be maintained with 2% ownership interest.

2 Management Company entity, passive income generator (PIG), setup to create passive income for children. Parents retain 100% control as managers. Children have no voting rights.

3 Management services agreements drafted and paid in full for next year's services before end of tax year.

4 Multiple customers with different ownership structures legitimizes the structure.

5 Passthrough income and management company and loss from real estate holding company optimized to net to zero on children's tax filings, so they don't pay any tax. This creates a situation where the parents' income is reduced by the amount of the management service agreements, and passive losses are utilized.

Success with any of these strategies lies in understanding the recourse debt risks and material participation rules. We always match the investment approach to your specific situation and risk tolerance.

Finding Your Strategy Match

I want to be clear about something important. These strategies are just a few examples of the powerful tax elimination approaches available. I've shared these particular ones because they're among the most effective and commonly used in our practice, but they're not the only options out there.

What makes these approaches particularly powerful is how they combine strategic leverage and income conversion elements with the incentives outlined in the tax code. There are other well-known strategies, but the strategies we've discussed here add unique dimensions to the conversation.

You see, there are plenty of strategies available, but it doesn't mean that you should implement them simultaneously. What typically happens is that clients find one approach that resonates with their situation, risk tolerance, and interests, and that becomes their specialty and where they focus their energy.

For example, the Charitable Holding Company is usually the kingpin when you're ready for a major liquidation event, like selling your business or a significant asset. Until then, you might focus on one of the other strategies we've discussed.

The most important thing is finding the right match for your specific situation. That's why proper implementation with expert guidance is so critical. It ensures that you're selecting and executing the strategy that aligns best with your goals, timeline, and risk comfort level.

The Power of Professional Leverage

One aspect of wealth building through tax strategy that often goes overlooked is what I call professional leverage.

While financial leverage multiplies your investment power, professional leverage multiplies your expertise and implementation capacity. And in my experience, this kind of leverage is just as powerful as financial leverage when it comes to eliminating taxes.

When you bring together a collaborative team, the impact on your strategies multiplies exponentially. I call this the Multiplier Effect of professional leverage.

Entity Structuring

Building the right entity structure is like constructing a custom home. You need an architect (your attorney), a general contractor (your CPA), and various specialists working in harmony. For example, when we create a multi-entity structure, we might use:

- An S-Corp to minimize self-employment taxes
- An LLC holding company to protect assets
- Operating entities for specific investments

Each piece works together, maximizing benefits while minimizing risk.

Charitable Strategies

This is where professional leverage truly shines. Implementing a Charitable Holding Company strategy isn't just about creating tax deductions. It builds a legacy. Success requires:

- Estate planners optimizing long-term benefits
- Tax professionals maximizing immediate deductions
- Legal experts ensuring proper structure
- Financial planners managing investment strategy

Advanced Investment Strategies

Whether we're talking about film financing, equipment leasing, charitable holding companies, or healthcare software RTU, each strategy becomes more powerful through professional collaboration:

- CPAs ensure compliance with tax law
- Attorneys structure entities and review contracts

- Portfolio managers integrate investments into your overall portfolio

Going back to Mark's story, his results were possible because he had the right team implementing those strategies in exactly the right way.

Each professional brought their expertise to the table, creating results far beyond what any single expert could achieve alone.

Mark's Transformation

Let me take you back to Mark's story and show you exactly what we did to transform his tax situation.

Mark was passionate about investing in real estate, but he faced a common challenge. Neither he nor his spouse could qualify as real estate professionals due to the time they spent running their primary business. This meant he couldn't use real estate losses to offset his substantial income.

But Mark had an advantage he hadn't considered. He had school-aged children.

Factoring this in, we created two new companies. One was for investing in real estate and another was for managing his business. The management company served legitimate functions, handling marketing operations that were previously expenses in his other businesses.

We structured ownership so that his children owned a percentage of both companies. Since they were minors, Mark could still maintain control through special custodial accounts.

The management company generated legitimate income through contracts with Mark's other businesses. Instead of all that income flowing to Mark's tax return, a portion now flowed to his children's returns based on their ownership percentage.

At the same time, they also received K-1s from the real estate holding company showing significant paper losses (thanks to depreciation and cost segregation strategies).

The passive income and passive losses essentially offset each other on the children's tax returns. The overall effect is that we reduced Mark's taxable income by approximately $400,000 that year. In his tax bracket, that translated to about $200,000 in actual tax savings.

This wasn't just a one-time benefit. This structure created ongoing tax advantages while building real wealth. More importantly, it gave Mark a framework for teaching his children about business ownership and financial responsibility from an early age.

Conclusion

The strategies we've explored in this chapter are proven pathways that have transformed how our clients build wealth. But to make them truly powerful, you need to implement them correctly.

Mark's frustration over watching nearly half a million dollars disappear to taxes each year wasn't unique. What transformed his situation was shifting his perspective to see the tax code as an opportunity rather than a burden, then implementing the right strategies with precision.

This is the transformation I want for you. Every dollar you currently pay in taxes represents capital that could be working for you instead. But to capture this opportunity you need to have the right guidance from the right team to ensure everything is implemented correctly.

In our next chapter, we'll really look into something we've been hinting about as incredibly important to these processes. That's documentation. You'll discover how proper documentation is like building a wall against IRS scrutiny, ensuring that every strategy you implement is both effective and defensible. We'll break down exactly what documentation you need, how to maintain it effortlessly, and how it transforms tax strategies from risky endeavors into confident wealth-building tools.

Chapter 5

Documentation: Your Shield Against IRS Scrutiny

Imagine getting an IRS letter in the mail. For most people, that's an instant alarming moment. They call their accountant in a panic, wondering if they've made a terrible mistake. Or they simply hope the problem somehow disappears.

But when my client John[4], a successful business owner making north of $800,000 annually, got that dreaded envelope questioning his activities, something different happened.

4 John is a fictional character. His story is based on the many clients I've worked with who faced similar challenges.

When he walked into my office that morning, he had a smile on his face.

"Show them everything," he said, pulling up our digital documentation system without hesitation. "We've got nothing to hide."

That moment perfectly captures what I've learned after years of helping successful professionals navigate tax strategies. When you build your approach the right way from the start, an IRS review isn't a threat. It's an opportunity to demonstrate your compliance.

From day one, we'd built what I call a bulletproof shield around John's tax strategy. Clear time logs tracking every hour he spent managing his investment and thorough financial reviews. Nothing fancy, just crystal-clear documentation showing exactly what he did, when he did it, and why it mattered.

Two weeks later, the IRS closed their review without a single adjustment. John kept his $500,000 in ordinary income offsets. What's even more important is that the process verified his absolute confidence in our approach.

A few days later, John said, "You know what's funny? All those hours I spent grumbling about keeping such detailed records? That documentation just paid for itself, many times over."

That's why I'm passionate about documentation. Think of it like building a fortress around your tax savings. Not because you're trying to hide anything. It's quite the opposite. You're creating clear documentation that proves you're doing everything right.

In this chapter, we'll explore how proper documentation can build a defensible wall around your tax strategies. You'll learn why most documentation efforts fail, how to ensure your tax positions are more than just defensible, and our unique approach to handling IRS inquiries.

From Burden to Shield

I've lost track of how many clients used to think that documentation was just a pointless red tape. Most people see it as nothing but annoying paperwork they have to deal with just to keep some random IRS person off their back.

I get it. After all, when you're running a successful business or managing a high-powered career, the last thing you want to think about is tracking every minute of your day.

But documentation isn't just about satisfying the IRS. It's your shield, protecting the tax savings you've rightfully earned by following the incentives built into the tax code.

This is why we approach IRS agents differently. We don't fear their questions. Instead, we welcome the opportunity to educate them.

The Education Advantage

Most tax professionals approach IRS inquiries completely backwards. They see it as a battle, stockpiling documents like ammunition and treating every communication as if they're under attack. Sound familiar?

Thousands of client interactions have taught me that the IRS isn't your enemy.

When an agent reviews your file, they're looking at complex tax positions they need to understand. They might see dozens of different tax strategies every week. Their job isn't to find problems. Rather, it's to verify compliance.

That realization transformed how we handle IRS inquiries. Instead of playing defense, we focus on telling our client's story through clear, organized documentation.

Every timelog, receipt, and document fits together like pieces of a puzzle, showing exactly why our tax position aligns with the code.

When we submit documentation, we make it crystal clear. No cryptic explanations or technical jargon, just straightforward evidence showing how our strategies follow established tax incentives.

The results speak for themselves. They provide faster resolutions, productive discussions, and better outcomes for our clients.

It's important to understand that this approach only works when your documentation is rock-solid. You can't explain your position effectively if your records have gaps or inconsistencies.

That's why we're obsessive about documentation from day one. Every strategy we implement, every deduction we take, every credit we claim comes with clear, timely records that support our position.

This approach gives our clients incredible peace of mind. They know that if questions ever arise, we're not scrambling to defend their position. Instead, we're ready to demonstrate exactly how their strategy aligns with the tax code's intentions.

Your Audit-Proof Framework

Now, you could ask me: "Jeremy, I'm doing everything legally, but *how do I prove it?*"

The key to audit protection isn't just having documentation. It's having the *right* documentation in the *right* structure. At our firm, we treat every tax return like it might get audited even though the chances are super low at less than 1-5%. This way, we make sure every tax detail is solid and follows IRS rules to the letter.

So, here are some strategies we use:

1. **Moving complexity off of Form 1040** - Most people pile everything onto their personal return, creating red flags that catch the IRS's attention. Things like home office deductions, for example, are pretty standard when filled through business return when categorized with other office expenses.

2. **Using entities like LLCs or S-Corps** - This strategy ties income and deductions to a balance sheet, unlike 1040 Schedules C, E, and F, which don't, and that's often why they catch the IRS's attention. By handling business activity through entities, clients can cut their audit risk by up to 80%.

But understand that we're not just creating random business entities. Each piece of your tax structure serves a specific purpose, fitting together like a well-designed puzzle.

This approach strengthens your asset protection, streamlines your reporting, and sets you up for long-term financial success.

When everything's organized logically, you can walk anyone, including an IRS agent, through your tax strategy step by step. It's about creating clarity, not complexity.

Building Your Documentation Shield

Documentation backs up your tax positions, keeps you in line with the tax code, and protects you in case of an audit.

But how can you build your documentation shield? After years of working with the IRS, I've learned what actually matters:

First Level: Your Foundation Documents

Think of these as your first line of defense. Focus on organizing those documents that tell your business story effectively, for example:

- Tax returns and supporting schedules
- Clean, organized bank statements
- Basic business records that show clear separation from personal activities

Second Level: Strategy-Specific Documentation

This is where things get interesting. Each tax strategy we implement needs its own specific support. It's about building a clear narrative that supports your tax positions. Here are some examples:

- For rental real estate owners, detailed participation logs that tell the story of your involvement
- For R&D credits, a clear development narrative showing how your work qualifies

- For private equity, records that demonstrate active engagement (material participation)

Third Level: Your Audit Shield

This is what separates good documentation from robust documentation. Most people never reach this level, but it's crucial for implementing advanced strategies with confidence:

Professional legal opinions that support your positions

- Clear audit trails for every major decision
- Strategic documentation of your business purpose
- Comprehensive records showing why each position aligns with tax code incentives
- Corporate formalities like maintaining operating agreements, annual meeting minutes, and secretary of state filings

By keeping detailed, accurate, and audit-ready documents, clients feel more confident to put tax strategies into practice, reducing risks and maximizing savings.

Implementation in Practice

Real-world tax documentation isn't about creating some complicated system that takes over your life. It's about building simple, effective habits that protect everything we're working to achieve.

Think about documentation like maintaining a high-performance car. You wouldn't wait until something breaks to check the oil or tire pressure. The same principle applies to protecting your tax strategy:

1. **Daily Habits:** Your business generates important information every day in decisions, expenses, investments. Each one is like a brick in the wall of your tax strategy. Take a few minutes each morning to record yesterday's key activities. That's it. No complicated processes, just quick, consistent documentation.

2. **Weekly Reviews:** Friday afternoons, when things are winding down, spend 15 minutes verifying your time logs and transaction categories. It's like checking your security cameras - a quick scan to make sure everything's in order.

3. **Monthly Checks:** This is your bigger-picture review. Are your entities compliant? Documentation complete? Team coordinated? Think of it as monthly maintenance on your car by catching small issues before they become problems.

4. **Quarterly Evaluation:** Now we're looking at everything strategically. Your documentation, strategies, and risk levels make sure all pieces fit together perfectly to protect your tax savings.

The beauty of this system is in its simplicity. You're not spending hours pushing papers around. You're capturing the right information at the right time, and we're ensuring it all works together to protect your wealth-building strategies.

Digital vs Physical: The Modern Shield

The days of dusty boxes filled with receipts are over. But here's where most people go wrong with digital documentation. They think randomly scanning documents into computer folders equals organization. It doesn't.

Picture your documentation system like a modern security system. Just like a security system needs cameras, sensors, and monitoring working together, effective digital documentation needs specific elements working in sync.

Cloud Storage Strategy

Your digital vault needs to be more than just storage space. It's like your command center. Everything is encrypted and organized logically to match your entity structure, backed up multiple ways, and instantly accessible when you need it. This is an additional service we provide to our best clients.

But don't toss those paper records in the shredder just yet. Some documentation still needs physical copies. It's about knowing which is which. Think of it like your wallet. Some things you're fine keeping digitally on your phone, but you still carry your driver's license in physical form.

Common Documentation Pitfalls

Most documentation failures don't happen because of complex technical issues. They happen because of a simple misunderstanding about who does what.

Here's what I mean. Many people underestimate their responsibility assuming that their professional team will handle all the documentation. The hard truth when it comes to documentation is that you can't outsource everything.

Your tax strategy is like a high-performance engine. Our team can build it, tune it, maintain it, but only you can put the fuel in.

That fuel is your daily documentation. Those quick time logs showing your participation. Those timely bank transfers. Those signatures on critical documents exactly when they're needed.

You might have brilliant investment strategies and perfectly structured entities. But miss one critical time log, mix personal and business funds just once, or try to recreate documentation after the fact, and suddenly your entire strategy is not that solid anymore.

The good news is that preventing these issues is surprisingly straightforward.

You don't need to become a documentation expert or spend hours organizing papers. You just need to handle your specific pieces of the puzzle. The ones only you can provide. Get those right, and everything else falls into place.

Conclusion

Remember how John smiled when that IRS letter arrived? That kind of confidence doesn't come from luck. It comes from preparation.

That's the transformation I see in clients who embrace proper documentation. They stop playing defense and start playing offense. They implement more powerful strategies, save more in taxes, and build wealth faster, all while sleeping better at night.

My challenge to you is to take a hard look at your current documentation system. Are you just checking boxes, or are you building a shield that protects and empowers your wealth-building strategies?

Documentation isn't about satisfying the IRS. It's about empowering yourself.

In the next chapter, we'll explore how the Virtual Family Office model brings all these elements together, creating a comprehensive framework for implementing advanced tax strategies. You'll learn exactly how to leverage professional expertise while maintaining control of your financial future.

Chapter 6

The Power of the Virtual Family Office

Imagine you're building your dream house. You've hired the best architect in town, an amazing contractor, and top-notch specialists for everything from plumbing to electrical work.

Sounds great, right? But the problem is that none of them talk to each other. The electrician has no idea where the plumber is putting the pipes. The contractor doesn't know what the architect changed last week.

Even though you're paying for the best, you're not getting their best work because everyone's working in their own bubble.

This is exactly what happens with most people's financial success team. I saw this with Eric[5], a client who'd built a thriving business from scratch. He had a great tax person, solid legal advice, and smart investment folks. But when he sat in my office, his frustration was clear.

"Jeremy," he said, pulling up his contacts, "I'm paying top dollar for all these experts, but I feel like I'm the only one trying to get them to work together. Half the time, they give me conflicting advice!"

As we dug deeper, I discovered a perfect example of this disconnection. Eric mentioned he had set up a trust based on his attorney's recommendation.

"That's great," I said. "What assets have you funded it with?"

He looked confused. "What do you mean 'funded'? I have a trust. My last guy told me to get one, so I did."

This is something I see all the time. People have excellent legal documents drafted, but the implementation piece is missing. Each professional is doing their specific job well, but they're working in isolation.

What Eric needed wasn't more experts. He needed coordination. That's why I help my clients put together what we call a Virtual Family Office (VFO). Think of it like a well-run business where you're the CEO,

5 Eric is a fictional character. His story is based on the many clients I worked with who faced similar challenges.

and your CPA acts as the COO and takes responsibility for results and ensures everyone is doing their part at the right time. Just as a COO coordinates different departments to achieve company goals, your CPA coordinates your professional team to optimize your financial outcomes.

The best part is that you get this high-level coordination without the massive cost of traditional wealth management.

In this chapter, I'll show you exactly how this works. You'll learn why the old way of managing wealth is falling short, how our approach fixes those problems, and most importantly, how you can use these same ideas to protect and grow your own wealth. Whether you're running a business or earning a high salary, what you're about to learn could completely change how you think about managing your financial future.

The Evolution of Family Wealth Management

The story of wealth management has much more to do with solving problems than with money itself.

It all starts back in the 1800s, with the Rockefeller family. Their wealth had grown so large that regular banks and advisors simply couldn't keep up. They needed something different.

When your wealth reaches a certain level, you're not just dealing with investments anymore. You're managing businesses, planning for future generations, navigating complex tax situations, all at the same time.

The Rockefellers understood this. So they created something new, the first family office. They brought together a dedicated team of professionals who focused on protecting and growing the family's wealth.

This model became the gold standard for ultra-wealthy families. For generations, if you had enough wealth, you'd build your own family office. You'd hire full-time accountants, lawyers, investment managers, all under one roof.

As times changed, a new kind of wealth creator emerged. Successful entrepreneurs, business owners, and investors needed sophisticated wealth management, but the traditional family office model didn't quite fit.

Why? Operating costs often exceeded $1 million annually, putting it out of reach for most successful families. Even if you could afford it, you were stuck with whoever you could hire full-time.

Some tried to solve this with multi-family offices by spreading the costs across multiple families. But new problems emerged:

- Limited access to specialized expertise
- One-size-fits-all solutions instead of tailored strategies
- High overhead costs that ate into wealth
- Difficulty implementing complex strategies quickly

The world of wealth was changing. These new wealth creators needed something different, something built for today's fast-moving, digital world.

The Virtual Family Office Revolution

The Virtual Family Office transforms everything about wealth management. Instead of limiting yourself to full-time staff under one roof, imagine having access to a network of top specialists who work together seamlessly to protect and grow your wealth.

What makes this approach revolutionary?

First, you get access to absolute top-talent in every field. Need an advanced tax strategy? You get the best tax minds. Complex estate planning? Top estate attorneys. Sophisticated investments? Expert analysts who live and breathe that specific type of investment. You're never limited by who happens to be on the payroll.

Second, the cost-effective structure changes everything. Traditional family offices charge millions annually because they're maintaining full-time staff whether you need them or not. With our VFO model, you scale services up or down based on what you actually need. Think of it like having an entire orchestra at your disposal but only paying for the musicians when they're performing your specific piece.

Third, and this is crucial, our implementation system ensures every professional works in perfect coordination. This means having the right expertise at the right time, working together to build and protect your wealth. Because we're not bound by traditional employment constraints, we can bring in the absolute best specialists for your specific situation.

The result is that you get sophisticated wealth management that was previously only available to the ultra-wealthy, but without the massive overhead costs and rigid structures that often make traditional family offices inefficient.

Inside the Virtual Family Office

Think about a championship sports team. Every player isn't just great individually. They understand exactly how to work together to win. That's exactly how our VFO pods work.

Each client gets their own dedicated team with all the expertise they need, working in perfect coordination.

At the center of each pod is the VFO coordinator. Remember that business analogy we used at the beginning of this chapter? It also works well here. Just as a great COO ensures every department head communicates effectively and executes on time, your VFO coordinator makes sure your financial team operates in perfect sync.

They're beyond just handling administrative tasks. They're the operational backbone ensuring every specialist knows exactly what the others are doing, preventing anything from falling through the cracks.

Now, let's look at the key players on your team:

1. **Tax Strategist/CPA** - Think of them as your strategic quarterback. But they're doing way more than tax returns. They're looking three moves ahead, spotting opportunities others miss, and designing strategies that work with your bigger picture. When they see a chance to eliminate taxes while building wealth, they're already coordinating with the rest of the team to make it happen.

2. **The Legal Team** - Most attorneys focus on their specific piece - drafting documents or handling contracts. Our legal experts see the whole board. They're crafting entity structures that not only protect your wealth but maximize every tax advantage. Every agreement, every contract, every entity they create fits perfectly into your bigger strategy.

3. **Investment Specialists** - These are like real estate agents or portfolio managers, bringing you opportunities that fit your parameters as they become available. They're building wealth with tax strategy in mind. This is something most people miss. The best investment opportunities often come with significant tax advantages. But you only capture these benefits when your investment team works in sync with your tax and legal experts.
4. **Estate Planning Experts** - This is the part of the team that ties everything together for the long term. This is way beyond basic wills and trusts - these specialists are architecting sophisticated strategies that protect your wealth for generations. They work side by side with your tax and legal teams to make sure every succession plan and wealth transfer strategy works perfectly with your overall protection plan.

Of course, these are just the core players on your team, though. But your team can expand or contract based on exactly what you need. Some clients might require additional expertise. They may need business managers for day-to-day operations, asset finders when you're looking for specific investment opportunities, bookkeepers to maintain pristine financial records, insurance experts to optimize your protection strategy, or specialized investment advisors for particular asset classes.

Because everything is so specialized now, you'll often need multiple attorneys on your team at various times for various purposes. The best part is that each of them has a narrow niche where they truly excel. Having a co-ordinated VFO means we bring in exactly the right legal specialists at exactly the right time, ensuring you always have the best expertise for the specific challenge at hand.

What really matters is how they all work together. When Eric came to us, he had great individual advisors. But those advisors weren't talking to each other. Each one had pieces of the puzzle but couldn't see the whole picture. Our VFO model changed that completely.

The Implementation Advantage

Here's how our VFO model fixed it:

1. **Coordinated Implementation**
    - Weekly team updates ensure everyone stays aligned
    - Clear documentation flows between all professionals
    - Proactive problem-solving before issues arise
    - Regular strategy reviews with all team members
2. **Systemic Accountability**
    - Clear responsibilities for each team member

- Documented timelines for all actions
- Regular progress checks and updates
- Digital systems tracking every step

3. Client Communication
    - Single point of contact for questions
    - Regular updates on progress
    - Clear explanations of complex strategies
    - Proactive notification of opportunities

Building Your Virtual Family Office Team

The power of a Virtual Family Office lies in the quality of its team members. But not just about finding great individual professionals. It's about finding professionals who know how to work together. We work with our clients to build their national (and, perhaps, international) team that suits their specific situation and needs. This definitely saves them a lot of time.

This is why we developed our peer review network. Every professional in our network has been vetted not just for their expertise, but for their ability to collaborate effectively.

We look For:

Expertise

- Deep knowledge in their specialty
- Proven track record of success
- Commitment to ongoing education
- Understanding of advanced strategies

Collaboration Skills

- History of successful teamwork
- Clear communication style
- Willingness to coordinate
- Proactive problem-solving approach

Implementation Focus

- Track record of execution
- Systems for documentation
- Commitment to deadlines
- Results orientation

The Quality Control Framework

If you're running a successful business or earning significant income, you probably know that having a great plan isn't enough. Execution matters more than anything.

You see, even the most brilliant tax strategy becomes worthless if the implementation steps aren't followed precisely, documentation isn't maintained properly, or deadlines are missed.

Our execution process is so detailed to make sure every strategy is implemented correctly and, most importantly, with quality! Yes, our quality control system is an essential part of our execution framework and acts as a safeguard throughout the implementation process, catching potential issues before they become problems.

First off, documentation standards are more than critical. Every action, decision, and strategy is captured and organized with military precision.

When you need to prove a position to the IRS or show exactly when and why you made a strategic decision, everything's right there, perfectly organized and instantly accessible.

Second, our review system works on multiple levels:

- Weekly team connections ensure all moving pieces stay aligned
- Monthly assessments catch potential issues before they become problems
- Quarterly deep dives let us step back and look at the bigger picture
- Annual planning sessions keep us moving purposefully toward your long-term goals

And finally, risk management is constant and proactive. We adapt strategies based on new opportunities or challenges before most people even know they exist. When tax laws change or new planning opportunities emerge, your strategy is already being updated.

This system protects your wealth and gives you peace of mind. You know your wealth is being protected by layers of sophisticated quality control that ensure nothing falls through the cracks.

Every strategy, every implementation, every decision is monitored, documented, and validated.

A Transformational Experience

Now, let's go back to our friend Eric. One of the first things we did for him was something that differentiates our approach from traditional advisors. We required him to send us all his operating agreements and trust documents, so we could review them and make sure everything aligned with his overall strategy.

Then we created something that's become the cornerstone of our practice: comprehensive entity maps. These visual diagrams show exactly how all the pieces of your financial structure should fit together. Think of it as the blueprint for your financial house, showing not just what entities you have, but how they connect and work together.

See Graphics on the Following Pages

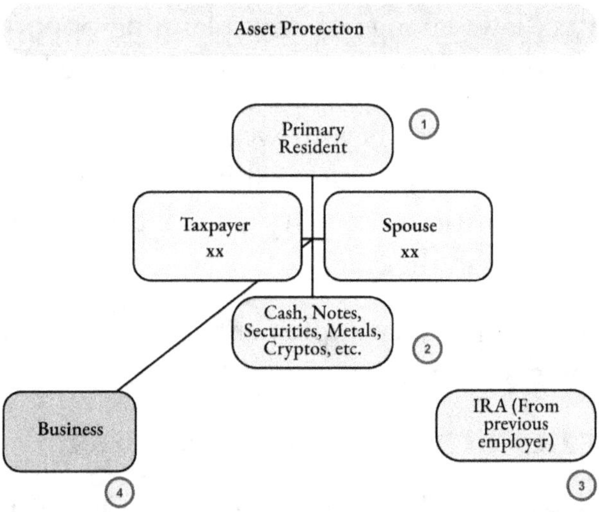

Footnotes

1. Assets above the Asset Protection shield are exposed to creditors and judgements in lawsuits. However, depending on state of residence, there may be protection for primary residence under "homestead" statutes

2. All assets must go through state probate process because there are no trusts

3. There may be better options for qualified retirement plan (QRP) assets from prior employers

4. Businesses without an entity must pay self employment taxes on top of income taxes and file Schedule C. That is the most audited form in human history and offers no asset protection.

Business Owner
December 2025

Proposed (Core Strategies) Structure

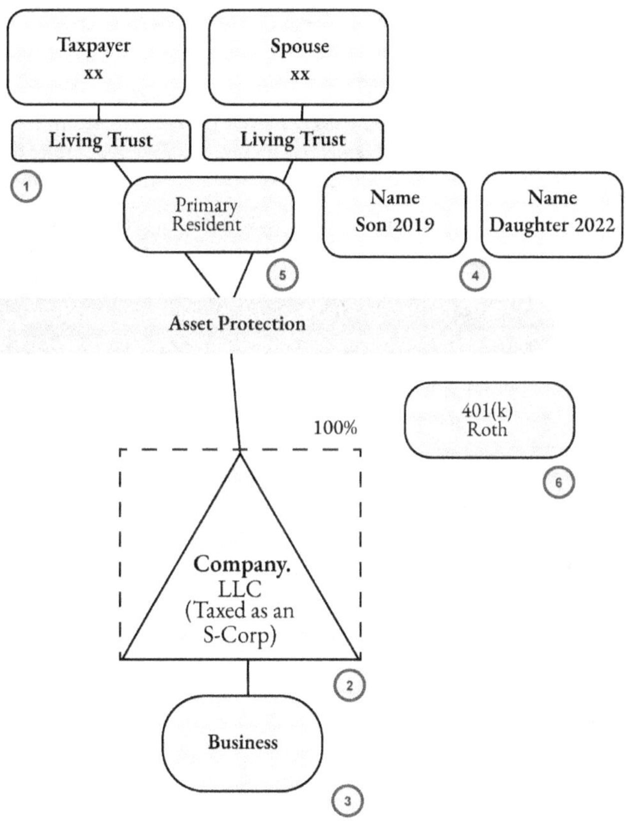

Footnotes

1. Revocable Living Trusts allow assets to avoid probate at end of life and 1 of 3 essentials to basic estate planning. The other 2: "pour over" will; medical power of attorney (POA)

2. Operating business setup as LLC taxed as S-Corp to eliminate self-employment taxes, increase asset protection, and reduce audit risk.

3. Accountable Plan allows your business to reimburse you for Home Office expenses, travel, meals, entertainment, and anything else that's ordinary and reasonable for your business' pursuit of income.

4. Hire your kids, so they have a budget for their personal expenses. The business gets to deduct the payments, and the kids do not pay tax on the first ~$15k.

5. Lease your home to your business for business planning meetings. The business gets to deduct it and you do not have to report the income if its less than 14-days.

6. Setup a 401k for your business to deduct ~$20k per year in investments.

Business Owner
December 2025

Proposed (Advance Strategies) Structure

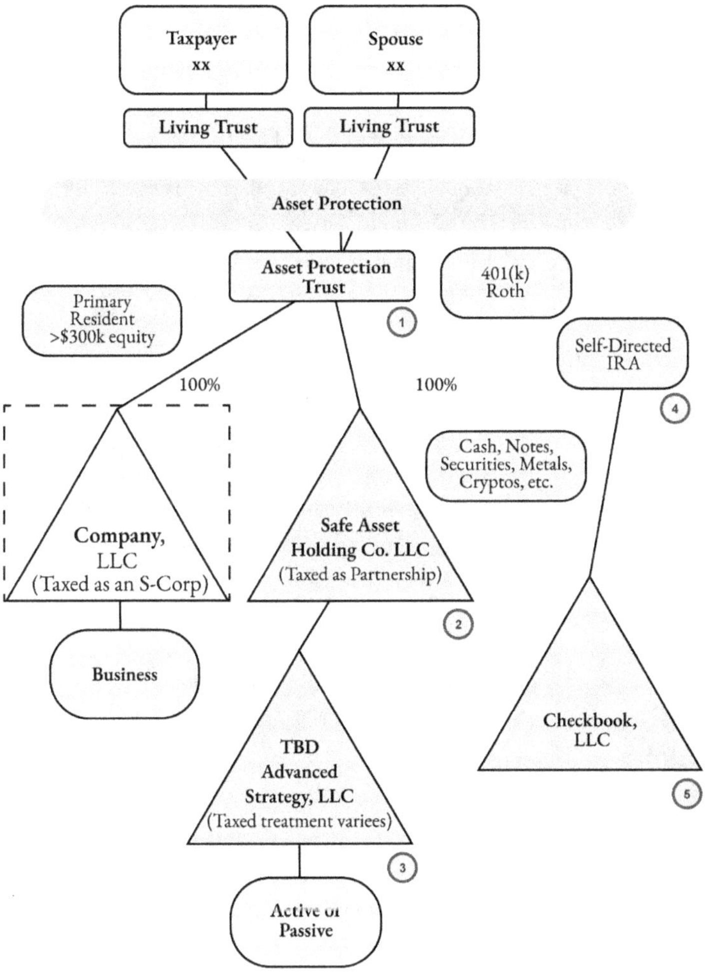

Footnotes

1. Irrevocable asset protection trusts protect home equity in excess of the "homestead" exemption in your state. Using a trust instead of an LLC allows the primary residence $500k capital gains tax exclusion to be preserved.

2. Holding company increases asset protection. It also decreases audit risk by moving the complexity related to advanced tax strategies onto a separate entity tax filing. Only put safe assets directly in the holding company;

3. Separate LLCs for each investment are used to protect the equity of other investments. Short-term rental real estate, Film Financing, Equipment Rental, Healthcare Software RTU, and other investments may qualify as an active activity with only 100-hours of material participation.

4. 401(k) or IRA unrelated to current employment may be rolled over into a self-directed IRA that allows an LLC to be created inside of it.

5. Checkbook, LLC may invest in nontraditional assets including private equity and crypto.

These entity maps optimize for four crucial elements:

1. **Tax Efficiency** - Ensuring your structure minimizes tax burden
2. **IRS Audit Avoidance** - Creating clean, defensible positions that reduce scrutiny
3. **Asset Protection** - Keeping your wealth safe from potential threats
4. **Estate Planning** - Creating structures for efficient wealth transfer

At our firm, we're experts in the first two areas, but we recognize that the latter two require collaboration with legal specialists. That's why we don't just hand clients a diagram and send them on their way. We start the process with our tax expertise, creating a framework that meets financial goals without triggering unnecessary tax consequences.

But the critical part is that there's no effective asset protection or estate planning unless those entities are properly set up and properly funded. I can't tell you how often I see clients with beautifully drafted trusts that own nothing, or multiple entities set up in an "implementation groove" where advisors create entity after entity, trust after trust, with nothing actually connected.

Every conversation I have with new clients revolves around these entity maps and the optimization of these four elements. Then we align these maps with a comprehensive tax plan that ultimately equates to long-term financial security. That's the essence of what we do.

Conclusion

Remember that dream house we talked about at the start? That's exactly what a Virtual Family Office builds for your wealth. But instead of walls, windows, plumbing, and electricity, we're creating something more valuable. Growth, protection, and lasting success.

When every expert knows their role and works as part of a coordinated team, your tax strategies synergistically align with your investments. Your legal structures protect your assets and reduce audit risk. Your estate planning preserves your legacy for multiple future generations. It's a transformational execution.

Take a moment and think about your own financial team right now. Are they really working together, creating a unified strategy? Or are they more like those independent contractors who never talk to each other?

If you're tired of being the go-between for your advisors, trying to make sense of sometimes conflicting advice, now you know there's a better way.

In the next chapter, we're going to look closely into advanced strategies for W-2 earners. You'll see exactly how the VFO model works even if you're not a business owner. We'll explore proven approaches to navigate the unique challenges of high W-2 income while building sustainable wealth through tax efficiency.

Chapter 7

Advanced Strategies for W-2 Income

You likely make six figures as an executive, physician, or tech leader, and every month, taxes take a big chunk of your hard-earned money.

Every dollar you "lose" means opportunities slipping away, dreams being delayed, wealth that could be building your future instead of funding the government.

Most of the brilliant professionals I work with, the ones leading and solving complex problems for major healthcare, technology, and energy companies, initially believe their W-2 status locks them into high taxes.

They've heard it from most CPAs they've consulted, "That's just how it works when you're a W-2 employee." But after years in this business, I can tell you that, no, this isn't necessarily how it works.

Let me introduce you to Steve[6], a finance executive from the Bay Area who thought the same thing. Working for a major brokerage house, he was earning a substantial $500,000 annual salary but watching nearly half of it disappear to taxes every year.

What made Steve's situation interesting was his role in alternative investments, specifically helping raise capital for Hollywood productions. When I explained how we could leverage his industry knowledge with a film financing strategy, something clicked.

Before I could even finish explaining it to him, Steve was already asking where to sign up. Why? Because it aligned perfectly with his existing expertise.

By investing $125,000 in a film financing strategy at the end of the year, Steve reduced his taxable income to zero. For the first time ever, he was actually excited to file his taxes early instead of extending. He had a substantial refund coming from all of his W-2 withholding.

With Steve's example, I want you to understand that your W-2 income isn't a limitation. It's actually

6 Steve is a fictional character. His story is based on the many clients I've worked with who faced similar challenges.

your foundation for implementing sophisticated tax strategies most professionals never discover.

The skills you've honed to make you successful in your career, like managing complex projects, driving results, and maintaining impeccable documentation are exactly what make these advanced strategies work.

In this chapter, I'm going to show you something that might seem impossible right now. I'll show you how to legally eliminate your tax burden while maintaining your successful W-2 career. You'll discover why traditional approaches fail high-income earners, how to leverage your professional expertise in surprising ways, and most importantly, how to implement strategies that align perfectly with your demanding career.

Breaking the W-2 Myth

W-2 income doesn't sentence you to a lifetime of high taxes. The truth is that the tax code doesn't care whether your income comes from a W-2 or a business. What matters is how you structure your activities and investments to align with the tax code's incentives.

This is where most people get stuck. They hear, "You need to be a real estate professional," or, "You need to start a business," and think it's impossible with their career. They're missing the point.

The real opportunity is in changing how you structure your investments and activities around your job.

Steve didn't need to quit his finance position to eliminate his taxes. He just needed to understand how to leverage specific sections of the tax code related to material participation. This was absolutely key for him.

What do I mean by material participation? It's how Steve could convert what would normally be considered a suspended passive investment loss into an active loss that could directly offset his W-2 income. This distinction is huge, and it's something most CPAs never explain to their W-2 clients.

For Steve, his deep knowledge of film financing made this a perfect fit. He could easily document his material participation in these investments because it aligned with his everyday expertise. The paper loss from the film financing investment became active rather than passive, allowing him to use it against his substantial W-2 income.

This is what transforms tax strategy for high-income professionals. It's an understanding of how to make the tax code work with your specific situation instead of against it.

The W-2 Strategic Framework

When you break down a successful tax strategy for W-2

earners, three core elements work together. Think of them as building blocks. Each one is powerful on its own, but transformative when combined properly.

1. **Material Participation Transformation:** You don't need to quit your job or become a full-time investor. The tax code gives us a precise pathway with the 100-hour rule. When you understand how to leverage this correctly, everything changes.

2. **Strategic Entity Structuring:** Many brilliant professionals try implementing advanced strategies without the right legal framework. It's like building a skyscraper without a foundation. You need clear separation between your W-2 income and investment activities, creating built-in audit protection from day one. Most advisors won't tell you or don't understand that audit risk is reduced dramatically when the complexity is moved off of Form 1040. Moving activities to business returns instead of piling everything onto your personal return reduces audit risk from around 5% to just 1%. That's a 500% reduction in risk on a percentage basis!

3. **Recourse Debt (Leverage):** Understanding the difference between recourse and non-recourse debt is huge. Recourse debt carries more potential risk, as we talked about earlier in the book. The investor needs to understand what that means for them.

What scenarios might require them to put in more capital? Are they comfortable with that level of risk? This risk assessment isn't just about protection. It's how we get the multiplying effect on tax deductions.

These three elements are like the legs of a tripod. Each one is powerful on its own. But when they work together? That's when W-2 earners start to see the kind of tax transformation they thought was impossible.

Material Participation: The Game Changer

When most tax professionals talk about material participation, they immediately focus on the 500-hour rule or 750-hour requirement for real estate professionals. They're missing something crucial in the tax code, which is a pathway that requires just 100 hours per year of participation, provided no one else in the activity exceeds your involvement.

This single insight changes everything for high-income W-2 earners. Instead of trying to squeeze 500 or 750 hours into an already packed schedule, you can focus on strategic investments requiring just 100 hours of documented participation.

But what makes this really work is that the hours need to be substantive, thoroughly documented, and aligned with your professional expertise. This is strategic involvement that the IRS recognizes as material participation. Also, the structure around the investment is incredibly important.

Making Hours Count: The Strategic Approach

For W-2 earners, every hour must be very productive. Here's how we make that happen:

1. **Align With Expertise**
    - Use your professional knowledge to qualify participation
    - Document how your expertise contributes to investment success
    - Invest in what you know and have interest in
2. **Strategic Time Management**
    - Schedule participation during off-hours
    - Use weekends effectively
    - Document travel time when appropriate
3. **Leverage Existing Activities**
    - Identify current activities that qualify as participation
    - Document professional research that benefits investments
    - Track relevant learning and development time

The Film Financing Advantage

Film financing under Section 181 offers the perfect combination of benefits:

- Requires only 100 hours of participation (if structured properly)
- Could count film research and review time
- Aligns with activities already enjoyed
- Provides substantial tax deductions
- Offers potential profit participation

Healthcare Software RTU: Strategic Alternative

For health-conscious W-2 professionals and/or in healthcare or technology, the Healthcare Software RTU strategy creates unique opportunities.

Think about combining your healthy habits and professional expertise with strategic software rights investments. This creates substantial upfront deductions while building potential ongoing income with:

- Clear alignment with professional expertise
- Substantial upfront deductions
- Ongoing income potential

Let me show you how this worked for another client, Dr. Jonathan. As a chief medical officer, he was able to align his healthcare expertise with software evaluation and implementation, easily meeting the 100-hour requirement while maintaining his full-time position.

The key was structuring everything properly from the start:

1. Entity Formation
    - Single-purpose LLC
    - Clear operating agreement
    - Separate banking and records
2. Documentation Systems
    - Digital time tracking
    - Activity logs
    - Professional contribution records
3. Implementation Framework
    - Clear participation guidelines
    - Regular review sessions
    - Audit protection protocols

With a $100,000 investment in the Healthcare Software RTU strategy, Dr. Jonathan reduced his taxable income by $700,000, creating about $350,000 in tax savings (federal and state combined).

And here's an interesting nugget about how we simplified the 100-hour participation requirement. Using technology, like an Apple Watch, can help track health data as part of the software evaluation process. These devices keep an audit log of time spent tracking health metrics and provide educational videos about the software, and it's all documented on the backend automatically. The company even provides you with an Apple Watch as part of the investment and built in app to automatically track your time towards material participation!

This means participants like Dr. Jonathan could easily meet the 100-hour rule without it becoming a burden on their already packed schedules. It's a perfect example of how the right implementation makes these strategies work for busy professionals.

Entity Structuring: Your W-2 Protection Shield

Many W-2 professionals try handling investment activities through their personal tax returns. That approach creates unnecessary audit risk. Doing so is like building a house on sand or with inferior materials. Eventually, things start to shift.

W-2 earners actually need more sophisticated structures than many business owners. Why? The IRS pays special attention when high-income W-2 professionals claim substantial deductions.

Your structure needs to stand up to that scrutiny. Let me show you how:

1. **Asset Protection Framework** - At the heart of this framework is what we call a Holding Company, which works like a family vault. You only put zero-risk assets directly into the holding company. For example, things like paper assets, Bitcoin, and ownership interests in other businesses. This creates a secure vault that keeps your most valuable assets completely protected and separate from any riskier activities. That's why I call it the "family vault", because it's where you keep the things you absolutely can't afford to lose.

2. **Special Purpose Entities** - Instead of throwing all your business activities into one big pot, we give each strategy its own compartment. Want to invest in equipment rental? That gets its own LLC. Looking at film financing? Another separate LLC. Each one operates independently, maintains its own clear paper trail, and keeps its activities distinct. This creates crystal-clear boundaries that protect each strategy while making documentation straightforward. This also makes the exit strategy cleaner and provides more optionality.

3. **Cash Flows** - This is something most people overlook, but it's absolutely crucial. Each entity gets its own dedicated bank account. No excep-

tions. When money moves, it moves cleanly and clearly between these accounts with a valid reason. This eliminates commingling risk. Think of it like having separate wallets for separate purposes. You always know exactly where every dollar belongs. This makes tracking simple, keeps everything clean for tax purposes, and ensures you never run into issues with mixed funds.

This might sound complex at first, but, once it's set up, it actually makes everything simpler.

You'll always know exactly where things stand, and, more importantly, you'll have real protection for everything you're building.

The Time Management Revolution

Most W-2 professionals look at these strategies and wonder how they'll find the time. With 50+ hours already committed to your career each week, adding more seems impossible.

But to be successful in implementing your strategies, you don't need more time. You need to make your existing time count strategically. It only takes two hours per week to meet the 100-hours of material participation you need to make advanced tax strategies effective.

If you add technology and systems to track these activities, you can make it easier to accomplish this without disrupting your existing career obligations. Specializing in the right strategy means that you already have an interest in the related activities, so they won't feel like work.

The Implementation Rhythm: Making Tax Strategy Automatic

The difference between success and failure often comes down to daily habits, not grand plans. I've seen brilliant strategies fall apart because someone thought implementation was just about the big moves. It's not. It's about building a rhythm that makes execution automatic.

Making implementation manageable

Think of implementation like training for a marathon. You don't just show up on race day and hope for the best. You build a training schedule that fits your life. That's exactly how we approach tax strategy execution.

Remember when I mentioned that meeting the 100-hour requirement breaks down to just about 2 hours per week? That's your target. Nothing more, nothing less.

Prioritize the work to do and decide how to fit that time into your schedule. When we're talking about hundreds of thousands of dollars in tax savings for only 100-hours of effort, it's worth it. Especially in ideal cases when the investment is something you're interested in.

If you're working with us, we'll provide direction. Then, all that really matters is getting priority tasks done between accountability meetings.

The Technology Advantage

We've moved way beyond paper logs and spreadsheets. Today's digital tools make implementation almost effortless. Mobile apps capture activities in real-time. Voice memos transform into structured documentation. Automated systems track everything that matters. The key is choosing the right tools and using them consistently.

The Multi-Level Review Process

Our team dedicates 10% of their time staying current with tax laws and implementation best practices. We do this to ensure every strategy works exactly as intended.

When you combine this expertise with your professional skills, tax strategy execution becomes another well-managed part of your business life.

The Accountability Factor

Regular accountability transforms good intentions into actual results. We don't just set up systems and hope you'll use them. We maintain consistent contact through calls, texts, and emails. Our virtual implementation meetings are working sessions where we review progress, clear obstacles, refine strategies, and get things done in real-time.

When you build these rhythms into your daily life, tax strategy execution becomes as natural as checking your email or returning phone calls.

Special Challenges for W-2 Earners

W-2 earners face unique implementation hurdles. When you're working 50+ hours a week in a demanding job, implementation becomes even more challenging.

Here's what makes it harder for W-2 earners:

1. **Time Constraints:** You can't just drop everything to manage investments or track business activities. Meeting participation requirements becomes a constant juggling act. Even scheduling team meetings gets complicated when your calendar is packed with back-to-back meetings and urgent deliverables.

2. **Documentation Demand:** W-2 earners face a higher bar when it comes to documentation. The IRS looks more closely at your activities, especially when you're claiming losses against substantial W-2 income. You need precise, detailed records of every hour spent and every decision made.

3. **Strategy Limitations:** Your W-2 position naturally restricts how actively you can participate in

other ventures. Unlike full-time business owners who control their schedules, you're working with limited, often inflexible hours. You need to meet the same requirements as someone with complete schedule control, but you have less flexibility.

Things can be a little more challenging for W-2 earners, but don't worry. There's always a path forward.

If you're struggling to meet that 750-hour requirement for real estate (which is not just about hours but also needs to be your primary activity), we don't just throw up our hands. We get creative. Could your spouse qualify as a real estate professional instead? If so, real estate losses that are normally passive could become active losses that offset your W-2 income.

And if that's not an option? Well, we could look at the short-term rental loophole. This works great with "Airbnb-style" properties where the average rental stays are less than seven days.

What's interesting about this approach is that it only requires 100 hours of material participation if it's actively managed. I've seen this work incredibly well for clients who are committed to real estate but can't hit that 750-hour threshold.

This step-by-step approach to finding the right solution is exactly what sets our implementation apart. We don't force you into a one-size-fits-all strategy. We adapt our approach to your specific situation, even with the constraints of a demanding W-2 career.

W-2 Employee
December 2025

Current (Before Strategy) Structure

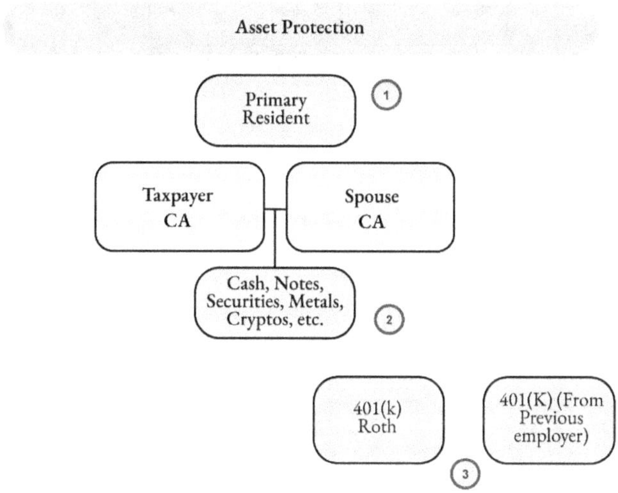

Footnotes

(1) Assets above the Asset Protection shield are exposed to creditors and judgements in lawsuits. However, depending on state of residence, there may be protection for primary residence under "homestead" statutes

(2) All assets must go through state probate process because there are no trusts

(3) There may be better options for qualified retirement plan (QRP) assets from prior employers

W-2 Employee
December 2025

Proposed Structure

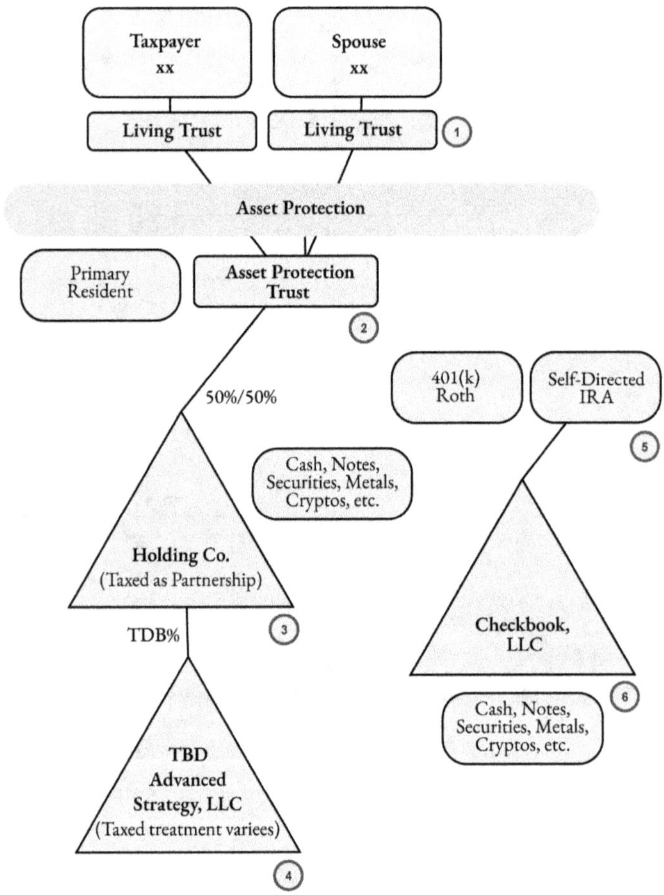

Footnotes

1. Revocable Living Trusts allow assets to avoid probate at end of life and 1 of 3 essentials to basic estate planning. The other 2: "pour over" will; medical power of attorney (POA)

2. Irrevocable asset protection trusts protect home equity in excess of the "homestead" exemption in your state. Using a trust instead of an LLC allows the primary residence $500k capital gains tax exclusion to be preserved.

3. Holding company increases asset protection. It also decreases audit risk by moving the complexity related to advanced tax strategies onto a separate entity tax filing. Only put safe assets directly in the holding company;

4. Separate LLCs for each investment are used to protect the equity of other investments. Short-term rental real estate, Film Financing, Equipment Rental, Healthcare Software RTU, and other investments may qualify as an active activity with only 100-hours of material participation.

5. 401(k) or IRA unrelated to current employment may be rolled over into a self-directed IRA that allows an LLC to be created inside of it.

6. Checkbook, LLC may invest in nontraditional assets including private equity and crypto.

Conclusion

As we finish this chapter, think about where you are right now. As an executive, physician, or tech leader, you're already managing complex initiatives and driving significant results.

Your attention to detail, your ability to implement systems, your commitment to excellence are exactly what make advanced tax strategies work.

Your W-2 income isn't holding you back. It's actually providing the foundation for building substantial wealth.

In the next chapter, we'll explore how business owners can scale up these same implementation principles. You'll discover how the methodical approach that works so well for W-2 professionals creates even more powerful opportunities when applied to business operations.

Chapter 8

The Business Owner's Tax Elimination Toolkit

It all started in the mid-70s, in Augusta, Georgia. The Masters Tournament was becoming huge. We're talking about thousands of golf fans flooding into this small Southern town. But there was a big problem. Augusta didn't have nearly enough hotels for all these visitors.

The solution? Local homeowners started renting out their homes to golf fans during the tournament. Pretty smart, right? But wait! It gets better.

The members of Augusta National Golf Club (who were pretty well-connected, by the way) looked at this situation and thought, *"Hey, these homeowners are helping solve a real problem for our community. Why should they have to pay taxes on this temporary rental income?"*

So they reached out to their friends in Washington and worked out a deal.

What started as a simple fix for Augusta's housing shortage turned into something amazing: the 14-day tax-free home rental rule. The best part is this rule isn't just for folks in Augusta anymore. It's for everyone. That means you, me, any business owner in America.

I'll give you some time to digest that. You rent your personal home to your business, your business gets to deduct the rental expense, and you don't pay a single penny in taxes on that income. How cool is that?

This is exactly what I want you to understand about the tax code. Most people see it as this scary, complicated monster designed to take their money. But that's not what it is at all. The tax code is more like a recipe book full of opportunities. Opportunities that were created to solve real problems for real people.

You know what gets me really excited? When I'm sitting with a client, and I see that light bulb moment. They'll look at me and say, "Jeremy, I can't believe I spent so many years thinking the tax code was my enemy!" But then comes the natural follow-up. "So...how do I actually use these opportunities to save money?"

That's exactly what we're going to cover in this chapter. Because knowing about tax strategies is one thing, but making them work for your business is something else, entirely. I probably sound like a broken record by now, but I'll say it again.

Implementation is everything.

I see it all the time. Business owners come to me, super excited about strategies they've heard about. Maybe it's the Augusta Rule or equipment depreciation or some other advanced strategy. They get the basic idea, but they're missing the key pieces that make these strategies actually work.

That's why I'm so excited about this chapter. I'm going to show you exactly how to use these strategies in your business. Not just the basic stuff every CPA knows about, but the sophisticated strategies that can completely transform your financial future. And, more importantly, I'll show you how to do it in a way that's both effective and audit-proof.

Think of this chapter as your practical guide. This is what I wish someone had given me when I first started learning about advanced tax strategies. The government has literally written us a playbook for how they want us to use their tax incentives. In this chapter, I'm going to show you exactly how to follow that playbook to transform your tax burden into wealth-building opportunities.

Balancing Today's Savings with Tomorrow's Wealth

The size of your tax savings isn't actually the most important metric of success. I know, coming from a tax strategist, that probably sounds strange. But what you do with those savings matters far more than how much you save.

Think about it this way: If you save $500,000 in taxes this year (and yes, that's absolutely possible depending on your income level, with proper implementation), you're essentially standing at a crossroads.

One path leads to immediate gratification. Maybe a new vacation home or an exotic car you've been keeping an eye on. The other path? That's where real wealth creation happens.

Here's what I tell my clients. Tax savings aren't the end goal. They're the beginning of your wealth-building journey. When we implement these strategies successfully, you'll suddenly have significant capital available.

Remember how we talked about the tax code being a playbook of incentives? Well, this is where that understanding really pays off.

Instead of just celebrating your tax savings (though you should definitely do that!), we need to think about how to use that capital in ways that align with those same government incentives.

So, here are some ways you can do that:

1. **Reinvesting in your business** - If you don't reinvest, there's no reason to celebrate. Reinvesting is the key to creating permanent tax savings. Strategy will not work if that doesn't happen. This often creates a multiplier effect, generating more tax advantages while growing your primary wealth engine and its valuation.

2. **Acquiring income-producing assets** - These are strategic real estate investments or business acquisitions that align with tax incentives.

3. **Building a diversified investment portfolio** - but done strategically, not just throwing money at the market or a private equity deal you heard about from a friend.

What makes this approach so powerful? When you direct your tax savings into these kinds of investments, you're creating a compounding effect.

Those investments generate more income, which we can protect using our tax strategies, creating more capital to invest...it's a glorious cycle.

Estimated Retirement Savings

If you invested your tax savings every single month between now and retirement, see how much additional you'd have in retirement

Estimated retirement savings
in 10 years, your investment could be worth: **$16,700,146**

INITIAL BALANCE	CONTRIBUTIONS	GROWTH
$2,200,000	**$3,340,540**	**$11,159,606**
13.00% of Total	20.00% of Total	67.00% of Total

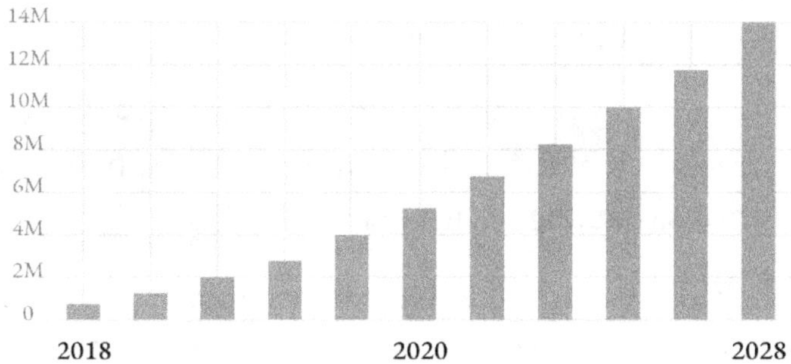

The main focus, and you probably know what's coming, is implementation. Having a clear plan for those tax savings before they hit your bank account. Understanding how each investment decision can multiply the benefits of your tax strategy.

The Strategic Foundation: Understanding Your Tools

You see, transforming tax savings into lasting wealth isn't just about making smart investment decisions. It's about having the right tools, and, more importantly, knowing how to use them properly.

I've sat across from countless successful business owners who've tried everything in the traditional playbook. They've invested in real estate, maxed out their retirement accounts, set up basic LLCs. Yet they're still writing massive checks to the IRS every year, often hundreds of thousands more than necessary.

They're missing the master key to tax elimination of proper implementation of all the essential elements. Not just some of them. All of them.

Now, let me share what I consider to be the Six Elements of Tax Efficiency:

1. **Entity Structuring:** This goes way beyond just forming an LLC and calling it a day. We're talking about building intentional structures that work together like a well-oiled machine with clear separation between activities and rock-solid documentation to back everything up. The right entities create the foundation for everything else we do.

2. **Strategic Deductions:** A lot of people either take deductions for granted or are afraid to claim them because they don't fully understand the rules. However, anything that's ordinary, necessary, and reasonable in the pursuit of income is deductible. Many clients miss opportunities in what they

perceive as "gray areas" like travel, meals, home office expenses. But with proper documentation, these aren't gray areas at all. They're legitimate deductions explicitly allowed by the tax code.

3. **Income Conversion:** This is one of my favorites, though it's a bit more abstract. We're way beyond just looking at how much you make. We're transforming how that income is classified and reported for tax purposes. One aspect of conversion involves the material participation rules we discussed earlier by strategically determining whether an activity is active or passive in a way that benefits you. Even something as simple as filing Form 2553 for an S-Corp election can convert self-employment income (subject to self-employment tax) into more tax-efficient business income. It's like turning lead into gold, except we're converting highly-taxed income into its most tax-advantaged form.

4. **Tax Bracket Optimization:** Most people don't realize that taxation is progressive. Everyone gets the benefit of the lower tax brackets before moving to higher rates, which cap out at 37%. When your strategy involves paying some taxes, we optimize which brackets that income falls into. We can also use family members' tax brackets strategically. For instance, business owners can hire their children, and the first $15,000 (approximately, as it's adjusted

annually for inflation) they earn isn't taxed due to the standard deduction. This teaches kids valuable skills while keeping money in the family.

5. **Elimination Strategies:** Here we focus specifically on permanently eliminating taxes on both cash flow and capital gains from your investments. Through strategic structuring and positioning, you can potentially create completely tax-free growth and returns. This is where strategies like tax credit optimization, opportunity zones, properly structured real estate investments, and charitable planning come into play.
6. **Strategic Tax Deferral:** This element allows you to increase deductions while postponing tax on a portion of your income. Think of deferral strategies like retirement accounts, installment sales, or 1031 exchanges. They don't eliminate taxes completely, but they give you control over when you pay them, which can create significant advantages.

Most business owners only tap into two or three of these elements. Think of it like trying to drive a car with only half its cylinders firing. You might move forward, but you're not getting the performance you should. Achieving zero tax requires all six elements working in harmony as your custom zero tax strategy.

Advanced Strategies That Transform Your Business

Those complex-sounding terms like "Section 181" and "Software RTU" that make most people's eyes glaze over? They're actually quite straightforward when you understand their purpose. Think of them as different plays in our tax code playbook, each designed to reward specific business activities that help grow the economy.

Here's a breakdown of some powerful strategies that can transform both your tax situation and your wealth-building potential:

1. **Film Financing:** This isn't just for Hollywood moguls. Section 181 of the tax code is a perfect example of government incentives at work. You can deduct production costs immediately while potentially generating ongoing income from distributions of profits. It's like getting paid to invest in America's creative industries.

2. **Leveraged Equipment Rental:** This strategy goes beyond simply buying business equipment. When implemented correctly, you can deduct the full cost of the equipment, including interest, right away. Think about that: Immediate tax savings plus a new revenue-generating asset!

3. **Software RTU (Right to Use):** Here's where things get really interesting. With proper imple-

mentation, you can turn a $100,000 investment into $700,000 in tax deductions. Plus, you may improve your own health and also benefit from a future liquidity event .

4. **The Augusta Rule:** This strategy is a perfect example of how understanding tax incentives can benefit both you and your business. You can rent your personal residence to your business for up to 14 days each year, creating tax-free income for yourself while giving your business a legitimate deduction.

5. **Charitable Holding Companies:** You're making a significant impact in your community while creating massive tax savings for yourself and heirs. That's exactly what this strategy allows. You transfer appreciated assets, maybe stock that's grown significantly in value or real estate worth far more than your purchase price, into a specialized holding company. Instead of facing hefty capital gains taxes when you sell, you get a charitable deduction, and the assets remain under your control to generate income for charitable purposes.

6. **Cost Segregation for Real Estate Investors:** Most people look at a building as one big asset. The tax code sees it differently. That HVAC system? The lighting? Even the flooring? They're all separate components with different depreciation

rates. By identifying and properly classifying these components, you can accelerate your depreciation deductions significantly.

But these are just some strategies. There are so many other incentives in the code that could leverage your tax strategies to another level.

Here's what this means in real terms: instead of waiting 39 years to get the full depreciation benefit from your commercial building, you could get a huge chunk of those deductions in the first few years. That's real money back in your pocket that you can use to invest in more properties or grow your business. In some cases, the related tax savings cover the downpayment on buying the property.

Speaking of family businesses...want a powerful way to keep money in the family while teaching valuable business skills? Consider hiring your children.

When structured correctly, this strategy offers multiple benefits. The wages you pay them (up to the standard deduction) are tax-free to them, but your business can still deduct the expense. Plus, you can help them start building their financial future by funding their own Roth IRA. It's a perfect example of how the tax code rewards family businesses that think strategically.

Finally, let's talk about R&D Credits, and no, these aren't just for tech companies or scientists in lab coats.

If your business is developing new products, improving processes, or creating software, you might be leaving money on the table. These credits are different from deductions because they directly reduce your tax bill, dollar for dollar. I've seen businesses save hundreds of thousands in taxes through properly documented R&D activities they were already doing.

But remember that each of these strategies requires proper documentation, correct timing, and strategic execution. When done right, they don't just save you taxes. They help build long-term wealth while rewarding activities that grow your business and benefit your community.

Just keep in mind that these aren't loopholes or gray areas. They're intentional incentives written into the tax code to reward specific types of business activities. The question isn't whether you should use them. It's how to implement them correctly to maximize their benefit for your business.

Entity Structuring: Your Financial Chess Board

You know what fascinates me about chess? It's about creating a strategic framework where each piece works together to protect the king and control the board. That's exactly how I want you to think about entity structuring.

I know this might sound complex at first. Most business owners I meet have a basic LLC or corporation, and they think that's enough. But what I've learned after years of implementing advanced tax strategies is that your entity structure is either working for you or against you. There's no middle ground.

Holding Company Structure

Think of a Holding Company as your chess board's king. It sits at the top, protected and powerful, holding your most valuable assets. When structured correctly as a partnership, it gives you incredible flexibility in how you allocate income while keeping your audit risk low. I love using holding companies for clients with multiple income streams or valuable assets that need protection from day-to-day business risks.

LLCs For Flexibility

LLCs are like your knights on the chess board. They can move in unique ways, giving you fantastic flexibility. Want to be taxed as a sole proprietorship today but switch to a partnership tomorrow? An LLC can do that. Need to protect your rental properties? LLC's got you covered. The beauty is in their adaptability. They can be anything for tax purposes but maintain their superior legal asset protection qualities.

S-Corporations for Tax Efficiency

S-Corporations? They're your bishops, moving strategically to slash your self-employment taxes. With an S-Corp, you can pay yourself a reasonable salary (yes, subject to payroll taxes) but take the rest as distributions that avoid self-employment tax entirely. It's completely legal, and, when documented properly, beautifully efficient.

C-Corporations for Growth

Think of C-Corporations as your rooks. They are powerful pieces for businesses planning significant growth. Yes, everyone talks about "double taxation," but C-Corps can retain profits and reinvest them at lower corporate tax rates or even loan excess cash to investment entities. Plus, they're ideal if you're planning to attract outside investors down the road.

Real Estate Investment Entities

For real estate investors, I love creating what I call "castle structures", or separate LLCs for each property, all protected under a holding company. It's like having multiple layers of defense protecting your assets. One property has an issue? It's contained within that LLC, leaving everything else protected.

Family Limited Partnerships (FLPs)

Think of FLPs as your queen on the chess board. It's incredibly powerful when used correctly. You maintain control while gradually transferring wealth to your family for estate tax avoidance purposes while retaining full control. It's beautiful in its elegance. This is one of my favorite moves.

Special Purpose Entities

These are like your pawns, but don't underestimate them. Each one is created for a specific purpose. Maybe it's for the equipment leasing strategy we talked about earlier, or perhaps it's for managing intellectual property. When positioned correctly, they're surprisingly powerful.

Multi-Entity Structure

Sometimes, you need a Multi-Entity Structure, which are multiple pieces working together in perfect harmony. High-risk operations stay separate from valuable assets, income flows strategically between entities, and everything works together to minimize taxes and protect what you've built.

Retirement Structures

This is your end game strategy. By combining the right entities with defined benefit plans or SEP IRAs, you can shield significant income from immediate taxation while building your long-term wealth. You can even set up an LLC inside of your retirement accounts to invest in alternative assets like A.I. tech startups.

Each of these structures has its place, but the real power comes from knowing how to combine them. Just like in chess, it's not about making one good move. Instead, the goal is to create a series of strategic positions that work together.

From Theory to Reality: Common Implementation Challenges

Let's do a quick imagination exercise. Christmas is around the corner, and you know it's time to start shopping for gifts. But instead of taking action, you keep putting it off, thinking, *"I'll get to it later."*

Fast forward to December 23rd, and you haven't bought a single thing. Now, you're rushing through overcrowded stores, grabbing whatever's left on the shelves, and paying way more than you planned because there are no options left. The perfect gifts you had in mind? They're long gone.

"Jeremy, what in the world does buying Christmas presents have to do with taxes?" you may ask me. I'll tell you that I see so many people try to implement complex tax strategies at the last minute. They're just like those last-minute holiday shoppers, stressed out, options limited, and usually paying more than they should.

One of the biggest obstacles I see is simply getting people to respond quickly enough to make these strategies work. You might have the perfect strategy in mind, but if you miss those critical end-of-year deadlines, that's real money left on the table.

Developing new habits is another thing that trips people up. I understand. Nobody wakes up excited about keeping detailed time logs or organizing receipts. But, by now, you already know that these aren't just paperwork exercises. They're the shield that protects your tax savings from IRS scrutiny. When you're converting passive losses to offset active income or proving material participation, those records are absolutely essential.

And technology actually makes this easier, not harder. We've got tools now that can help track everything from time spent on business activities to organizing receipts. But even the best tools only work if you use them consistently.

The good news is that these challenges aren't unique to you. And they are completely manageable with the right support system and approach.

But don't worry. This isn't something you have to figure out alone. That's why we have regular accountability meetings with our clients and build systems to make documentation easier. At the end of the day, even the most brilliant tax strategy is only as good as its execution.

Conclusion

As we close this chapter, I want you to have something clear in mind: achieving zero tax isn't about finding loopholes or taking shortcuts. It's about understanding how the tax code really works and using it exactly as intended to reward certain behaviors with tax benefits that can be transformed into lasting wealth.

The tools are available. The strategies are proven. The only question is if you are ready to implement them properly.

In the next chapter, we'll explore how to build your tax elimination timeline, showing you exactly how to sequence these strategies for maximum impact. You'll learn how to create a customized implementation schedule that turns tax elimination from a yearly scramble into a predictable process.

Chapter 9

Building Your Zero Tax Timeline

Time is the one resource you can't buy more of. Yet, every December, my phone starts ringing with the same urgent request: "What can I do to save on taxes before the year ends?"

These calls come from brilliant entrepreneurs and successful executives. They're masters at running businesses, closing deals, and generating wealth. But they've fallen into a trap that costs them hundreds of thousands in unnecessary taxes year after year. They wait too long to act.

And this is not an uncommon situation. So many clients I've helped used to have that urgent realization as December approaches. "I need to do something about taxes." Time is definitely something that trips people up.

You might be thinking, "Okay, Jeremy, I understand starting earlier is better. But why does timing matter so much?"

Would you try to plant a garden today and expect a harvest a week from now? Of course not! You know that it needs planning and consistent care throughout the seasons. Tax strategy works the same way.

Tax elimination isn't a one-time event like filing your tax return. It requires careful timing, strategic sequencing, and methodical implementation.

When you truly understand this, everything changes. You stop seeing tax strategy as something you do once a year and start seeing it as a continuous process that builds wealth over time. It's like the difference between trying to get healthier by working out once a year versus maintaining a consistent fitness routine.

In this chapter, I'm going to walk you through exactly how to build your zero tax timeline. We'll explore why timing transforms strategy from theory to reality, how to sequence your implementation for maximum impact, and, most importantly, how to create a rhythm that turns tax elimination from an annual scramble into a predictable process.

The Psychology of Time in Tax Planning

Let's address something that costs Americans billions in unnecessary taxes every year: the "I'll handle it later" mindset. Remember our little exercise about Christmas last chapter?

Most people treat tax planning like a yearly event. It's something to think about when returns are due or during that panicked December rush.

I know we're all busy. Whether you're working 50+ hours a week or running your successful business, time is short for all of us. But continuing to push your tax strategies to "next quarter" or waiting until December to implement them could be really expensive.

Here's why:

- Critical deadlines have already passed
- Implementation gets rushed, increasing errors
- Documentation becomes harder to reconstruct
- Strategic opportunities are missed entirely

But more importantly, you lose the compounding effect of properly timed strategies. Every month of delayed implementation is another month of lost tax savings.

Your Zero Tax Strategy

The faster you move, the better the results. But this is not just about moving fast. It's about moving strategically. So, how do you start?

In my approach, we separate the process into two distinct phases: strategy development and implementation. Strategy development always comes first. It's a really in-depth look at your situation before we take any action.

Our strategy development process transforms how our most successful clients approach their taxes. This process helps us create efficient strategies that match their specific goals before we ever implement a single tactic.

We start with some basic steps:

1. **Gather and Analyze Client Information:** That means digging deep into your tax returns, financial statements, and current entity structures. We hunt for hidden opportunities and inefficiencies that most people miss entirely.
2. **Draft Entity Maps and Initial Findings:** Imagine having a clear visual representation of how your financial structure could work to eliminate taxes. It's like having a GPS for your tax strategy, showing you exactly where you are and the best route to where you want to go.

3. **Present Initial Findings:** Our next step is presenting the entity maps and findings for the client in a collaborative meeting. During this session, we go through a detailed discussion to understand the client's vision, answer their questions, and make sure everything aligns with their goals.

4. **Alignment:** Once we have this foundation, we can start selecting the most powerful strategies for your situation. We focus on creating a synchronized system where each strategy enhances the others. This involves several live consulting sessions with experts in various fields.

5. **Implementation:** When everyone is on the same page, we begin the process of bringing the strategy to life, one priority at a time.

If you're highly engaged, the strategy development process and implementation of the top priority may be completed in as little as 30 days. But, for most clients, it will take longer.

Speed isn't what is most important. Thoroughness and proper execution are. Of course, we'd like to have sufficient time to do it all right the first time, but understand that some new clients do not have that luxury when getting started late in the year.

Understanding the Milestones

Your journey to zero tax is more than just checking boxes on a timeline. Each milestone in this process builds on the previous one, creating a tax-free future that's both sustainable and bulletproof against IRS scrutiny.

Think of each phase as building blocks in your financial fortress. Skip one, rush through another, and the whole structure becomes vulnerable. But get them right and in the right order, and you're creating something virtually unshakeable.

Phase 1: Strategy Development

Timing is everything. The first weeks lay the groundwork for your entire tax-free future. Here, we're looking for hidden opportunities that most people miss entirely. You'll see exactly how much you can save, which strategies will get you there, and the specific sections of the tax code that make it all possible. Important deliverables include detailed entity maps and a comprehensive tax plan document. This phase may be completed in as little as 30-days for highly engaged clients.

Phase 2: Strategy Implementation

This is where theory transforms into reality. Everyone gets their marching orders. Clear, specific, and timed for maximum impact.

We're working as a Virtual Family Office (VFO) team to set up your entities, create audit-proof documentation systems, connect you with investment specialists, and run our first real-world tests of your strategy. Think of it like test-driving a high-performance vehicle. Everything needs to work perfectly together.

Some details on how it goes:

1. **Action Item Assignment** - This step is crucial. You'll know exactly what needs to happen, when it needs to happen, and who is responsible.

2. **Entity Formation and Restructuring** - Here we focus on making the plan real. We're collaborating with your asset protection and estate planning attorneys on setup of new entities and trusts and/or modifying existing ones, and making sure everything is working together tax efficiently. This creates the foundation for your zero tax future.

3. **Documentation Preparedness** - You know I've said this before, and I can't stress this enough, but proper documentation is what makes the difference between hoping the IRS accepts your position and knowing they will. We're creating audit-proof records for everything.

4. **Initial Implementation Reviews** - Our first implementation review. Think of it like a test drive of your new tax strategy. We're making sure that all

action items have been completed, and everything is working exactly as planned and addressing any adjustments needed.

Phase 3: Strategy Maintenance

Getting to zero tax is only half the battle. Staying there requires consistent attention. It's like maintaining a healthy weight. You don't just diet for a month and expect results to last forever. It requires forming new habits. We're looking at quarterly check-ins, annual reviews, and constant monitoring for new opportunities as tax laws evolve.

Thoroughness beats speed every time. Each milestone serves a specific purpose in getting you to zero taxes and keeping you there.

The Four Critical Timelines You Must Master

When I first started helping clients eliminate their taxes, I thought there was just one timeline to worry about. The tax year. Boy, was I wrong. What I discovered, and what I want to share with you now, is that true success requires mastering four distinct but interconnected timelines.

1. Calendar Year Planning

This is your strategic foundation, and it's about much more than just watching dates on a calendar. Think of it as your master blueprint for the year. The time remaining in your calendar year often determines whether a strategy can deliver its full benefits or not.

Take asset acquisition, investments, or charitable contributions, for example. These opportunities have hard deadlines. Miss December 31st, and the potential tax benefits for that year are gone forever. I've seen too many people leave hundreds of thousands of dollars on the table because they didn't respect this timeline.

2. **Tax Year Optimization**

This is where things get interesting. Your tax year timeline might not match the calendar year, and that creates unique opportunities. But it also requires careful planning. We're not just thinking about when to file. We're strategically timing every move to maximize your benefits.

This timeline is particularly crucial when we're dealing with entity structuring or implementing complex strategies. Sometimes, extending your tax filing deadline isn't procrastination. It can be strategic positioning to give us the time needed to implement everything properly.

3. **Strategy-Specific Timing**

Each strategy has its own unique timeline requirements. Creating a charitable holding company has different timing needs than implementing a real estate investment strategy. Understanding these requirements is crucial because they often involve multiple professionals like tax advisors, attorneys, and valuation specialists who all need to coordinate perfectly.

Think of it like a complicated dance where everyone needs to move in perfect sync. Miss one step, and the whole performance can fall apart. That's why we break down complex strategies into smaller, manageable steps and carefully coordinate everyone involved.

4. Personal Implementation Rhythm

This is where everything comes together, and, honestly, it's often the make-or-break factor in successful tax elimination. This timeline is about creating your personal rhythm of execution and how you'll stay on top of documentation, decision-making, and regular reviews.

This is completely customizable to you. While we need weekly activity tracking and monthly strategy reviews, how we structure those depends on your schedule and working style. We maintain consistency without letting it become overwhelming.

Success comes from maintaining clear communication throughout the process, being adaptable when circumstances change (because they will), and ensuring every step is properly documented and reviewed.

What I want you to take away from this is simple. Tax elimination isn't a one-and-done event. It's a carefully orchestrated process where timing is everything. Master these four timelines, and you'll have the framework you need to eliminate taxes permanently, not just temporarily.

Building Unstoppable Momentum

You know, something I've understood after all these years in this industry is that the key to maintaining momentum has much more to do with working smarter than working harder. And by working smarter, I mean having a structured rhythm of accountability.

We drive the process for you. It's a done-for-you solution. After each strategy session, we follow up within 48 hours with a recording of that meeting, a detailed summary, and, most importantly, a clear list of action items for everyone involved.

Before concluding each meeting, we always do two critical things:

1. Schedule the next meeting
2. Review action items to ensure everyone knows exactly what they're responsible for

This approach creates clear accountability. Everyone on the team, including you as the client, has specific responsibilities between meetings. While we handle most of the heavy lifting, there are certain things only you can do:

- Locating specific documents
- Making key decisions about your strategic focus
- Determining which asset classes align with your goals.

For most clients, meeting every two weeks during the first several months works best. We've found that going longer between meetings creates issues with remembering context and reduces motivation. This consistent rhythm keeps everyone engaged and moving forward.

Once the strategy is implemented, we don't just disappear. We maintain regular check-ins to ensure everything stays on track. One of the most important aspects of these ongoing meetings is preventing unplanned actions, like selling an asset without consulting us first. Things will always go better when you share what you're thinking before making major financial moves.

Think of this rhythm like compound interest for your tax strategy. Small, consistent actions build up to massive results over time. Each meeting, you're building momentum that carries you toward your goal of zero taxes.

Conclusion

You've seen how timing transforms tax strategy from theory into reality. But knowing isn't the same as doing. Success in eliminating taxes doesn't wait for perfect timing. It starts with taking action today.

Time is the one resource you can't get back. But, with the right timeline, implementation rhythm, and team, you can transform your tax situation permanently.

In the next chapter, we'll explore how to create your multi-generational legacy, showing you exactly how to ensure your tax strategies create lasting impact for generations to come. You'll learn how to build systems that protect and grow your wealth long into the future.

Chapter 10

Creating Your Multi-Generational Legacy

Legacy isn't what you leave behind. It's what lives on through generations. And that's something the Andersons[7] know very well.

I've been working with the Anderson family for a long time. They'd been in Seattle for generations, steadily building an impressive portfolio of apartment buildings. On paper, they had everything figured out. They had substantial real estate holdings, successful business operations, and two adult children who'd naturally fallen into the family business.

Like many successful families, they'd focused on build-

7 The Andersons are fictional characters. Their story is based on the many clients I worked with who faced similar challenges.

ing wealth without fully considering how to preserve it for future generations. But when they finally started digging into the estate tax implications, they didn't like what they found.

What happened next is why legacy planning means implementing the right structures to protect and transfer it effectively.

Through a carefully designed family limited partnership structure, we created a framework that allowed them to gift their interests in the holding company at a discount to their sons over a 15-year period. This strategy was brilliant because we used strategic business valuations and discounts for lack of control and marketability, and many of these gifts weren't even reportable. We spread them over such a long time horizon that they didn't count against their lifetime estate and gift tax exemption.

This meant the parents maintained control with just 2% ownership while systematically transferring wealth to the next generation. Most people don't realize that strategies implemented now can be grandfathered in, protecting your legacy from future tax changes if you act before that deadline.

This family's story captures the essence of what effective legacy planning looks like. Create structures that protect wealth while empowering future generations to build upon what you've created.

In this chapter, we'll explore how to build a legacy that transcends generations. You'll discover why most legacy plans fail, how to implement strategies that protect your wealth for decades to come, and, most importantly, how to create lasting impact that goes far beyond financial success. We'll examine the critical elements that transform good intentions into multigenerational results, and you'll learn exactly how to implement systems that ensure your legacy endures.

The Legacy Paradox: Beyond Financial Success

The size of your estate has little to do with how successfully it transfers to the next generation. I've seen modest estates create powerful multigenerational impact while massive fortunes dissolve within a single generation.

Most legacy plans fail not because of poor strategy but because they focus too much on *just* passing down money. They treat estate planning like a technical exercise rather than what it really is , which is a blueprint for family success across generations.

This has real, practical implications:

- Without proper structure, even substantial financial success becomes vulnerable
- Tax strategy becomes your tool for creating generational impact

- Family values act as the foundation that keeps wealth intact
- Implementation determines whether your wealth brings your family together or pulls it apart

This is why traditional estate planning often falls short. It addresses the technical aspects of wealth transfer but misses the crucial elements that make legacy sustainable.

Understanding the Modern Legacy Challenge

There's something I've been watching closely, and it changes everything we thought we knew about estate planning. For years, we were staring down the 2026 estate tax cliff. The exemption was set to get cut roughly in half, and families with real wealth were going to get hit hard. The urgency was real, and the strategies we put in place to get ahead of it were absolutely the right move.

But here's the update: the One Big Beautiful Bill, signed into law on July 4, 2025, permanently raised the estate tax exemption to $15 million per individual, $30 million for married couples, starting January 1, 2026, with annual inflation adjustments. No sunset. No cliff.

This is not a reason to stop planning. Congress can change the law again. The 40% federal estate tax rate still applies to everything above the exemption, and most of that wealth isn't sitting in a bank account. It's tied up in businesses, real estate, and investments built over decades. When the bill comes due, families are often forced to sell what they spent a lifetime building.

The window to act wisely is open right now. The best structures are built before you need them, not after. But the impact goes beyond just numbers. Most successful people don't have their wealth sitting in cash. It's tied up in businesses they've built, real estate they've acquired, or investments that have grown over time. When the estate tax bill comes due, families often face tough decisions about what to sell off to pay the taxes.

But the impact goes beyond just numbers. Most successful people don't have their wealth sitting in cash. It's tied up in businesses they've built, real estate they've acquired, or investments they've grown over time. When that estate tax bill comes due, families often face tough decisions about what to sell off to pay the taxes.

I've seen people breaking up family businesses or selling properties that had been in the family for generations because they needed cash for the tax bill. The tax doesn't care if your assets are liquid or not. It's due nine months after death, period. Without planning ahead, this can really disrupt everything you've worked so hard to build.

That's why we implement strategies like strategic gifting, family limited partnerships, and properly structured life insurance policies. These approaches can either eliminate the estate tax burden entirely or create tax-free liquidity to pay any taxes without having to sell family assets.

But that protection only works if you act *before* the deadline. Today's wealth creators face unique obstacles:

1. Economic complexity that grows by the day
2. Technology that transforms faster than ever
3. Shifting social dynamics that impact wealth transfer
4. Growing challenges in moving assets between generations

The solution means implementing comprehensive strategies that address both the financial and human elements of creating a lasting legacy.

The Four Pillars of Lasting Legacy

After years of implementing legacy strategies with successful families, I've observed some patterns.

These patterns form what I call the Four Pillars, which are the essential elements that consistently create lasting impact. When these pillars work together, they create a foundation strong enough to support wealth across generations.

The Financial Structure

Most people think legacy planning starts with estate documents. But the foundation of lasting legacy begins with strategic entity structuring.

Think about what the Andersons discovered. They had accumulated impressive wealth through apartment buildings over multiple generations. But it wasn't until we implemented a comprehensive family limited partnership structure that their legacy became secure.

We developed a fifteen year plan to systematically transfer ownership while maintaining parental control with just 2% ownership.

We didn't just transfer assets. We created a framework that:

- Protected wealth from excessive taxation
- Maintained family control over assets
- Created clear succession pathways
- Built in flexibility for future changes

This wasn't just about avoiding estate taxes. It was about creating a structure that would support family success for generations.

Family Education and Governance

Money without education often creates more problems than opportunities. That's why family meetings have become central to our implementation process.

Think of these meetings as your family's board of directors sessions. They serve specific purposes:

- Building practical knowledge about wealth management
- Developing financial literacy across generations
- Creating clear frameworks for family decisions
- Establishing shared values and mission

These meetings become the training ground where future generations learn not just about managing wealth but about carrying forward your family's values and vision.

Value Transmission: The Hidden Key

Values transfer more reliably than valuables. This isn't just philosophy. It's practical reality.

When we implement charitable holding companies for clients, we're doing more than creating tax advantages. We're building frameworks that:

- Align wealth with family values
- Create meaningful philanthropic impact

- Build shared purpose across generations
- Maintain family unity through transition

But the crucial element is documentation (Yes, I've said it again, because it's that important!). Every decision, every value, every intention needs to be clearly recorded and communicated. This creates clarity that prevents future confusion.

Professional Integration: Making It Work

No single professional has all the answers in today's complex environment. Success requires a coordinated team working together seamlessly. Here's how we make that happen:

Clear Communication Protocols:

- Regular team updates
- Structured review sessions
- Documentation sharing systems
- Coordinated implementation timelines

Strategic Timing:

- Meeting critical deadlines
- Aligning implementations across disciplines
- Coordinating team actions effectively
- Maintaining consistent progress

Powerful Legacy Planning Strategies You Need to Know

When it comes to legacy planning, focusing on a single "perfect" strategy rarely works.

Success comes from weaving together multiple powerful tools that complement each other. After working with hundreds of families, I've identified five strategies that consistently transform family legacies.

The Magic of Charitable Holding Companies

While most people see charitable holding companies purely as vehicles for philanthropy, they're actually much more powerful than that. These structures allow you to transfer appreciated assets, avoid immediate capital gains taxes, and maintain control over how your wealth creates impact.

Think of it as building your own family foundation but with significantly more flexibility in how you manage and direct the assets when a non-grantor inheritance trust is added with a strategic investment LLC. This creates a structure that aligns perfectly with both your financial goals and your family's values.

Strategic Gifting: More Than Just Writing Checks

The IRS actually provides incredible opportunities for strategic wealth transfer. They're practically inviting you to use them.

Each year, you can gift specific amounts completely tax-free to as many people as you choose. There are many tools available to elevate this opportunity. By using the appropriate tools, we can amplify these gifts, moving significant wealth while minimizing estate taxes.

What makes strategic gifting particularly powerful is that you get to witness your legacy taking shape while you're here to guide and adjust it. Instead of hoping your plans work out someday, you see the impact unfold in real time.

The Power of Irrevocable Trusts

These aren't just legal documents; they're protective structures that shield your assets from creditors, lawsuits, and estate taxes. The protection they provide actually grows stronger over time.

Whether you're using an irrevocable non-grantor inheritance trust, life insurance trust to handle future estate tax bills or establishing a dynasty trust to protect wealth across multiple generations, these structures create lasting protection that becomes more valuable with each passing year.

Business Succession: Beyond Just Passing the Torch

If you wait until you're ready to retire to think about succession, you've waited too long. Smart succession planning uses tools like family limited partnerships (FLPs) and strategic gifting to transfer ownership gradually while maintaining control.

The secret? It's not just about transferring ownership. It's about transferring knowledge, relationships, and responsibility in a way that sets the next generation up for success.

Estate Tax Avoidance: Playing Chess, Not Checkers

Estate tax avoidance is all about understanding and using the incentives built directly into the tax code. When you align your planning with what the government wants to encourage, whether through spousal portability, charitable remainder trusts, or strategic real estate planning through cost basis "step-ups", you're maximizing opportunities the system provides.

The real power emerges when these strategies work together. A charitable holding company might connect with your gifting strategy, which then supports your succession planning, all while minimizing estate taxes.

It's about creating a coordinated approach where each strategy strengthens the others.

What Really Matters in Legacy Planning?

I could present tons of strategies for legacy planning here, but the elements that resonate most deeply with successful families aren't always what you'd expect.

After years of helping families create lasting legacies, I've noticed some key elements that truly matter.

1. **Family Security:** It's not just about leaving money behind. It's about creating systems that protect and nurture your family's success long after you're gone. That's why tools like irrevocable trusts and charitable holding companies resonate so deeply. They provide multi-generational security everyone is looking for.

2. **The Tax Efficiency Factor:** Nobody wants to see their hard-earned wealth eaten away by unnecessary taxes, especially now that we know how much fraud, waste, and abuse there is in that system. When I show families how tools like dynasty trusts or strategic gifting programs can help them transfer wealth efficiently, their eyes light up. This is being smart about how wealth moves between generations.

3. **Creating Meaningful Impact:** This one is fas-

cinating. The most fulfilled families are passionate about creating impact. Whether it's through charitable holding companies or donor-advised funds, they want their success to make a real difference in the world. Build a legacy that matters not just a fortune that lasts.

4. **The Power of Clarity:** Want to know what successful families love most about their legacy plans? Clarity. They don't want complexity. They want straightforward, actionable plans they can understand and explain to their children. When everyone knows their role and responsibilities, great things happen.

5. **Next Generation Engagement:** The best legacy plans actively involve the next generation. It's not enough to create brilliant strategies. You need to prepare your heirs to continue them. That's why family meetings and structured mentorship programs are so crucial.

6. **Alignment with Your Values:** Your legacy should reflect who you are, not just what you own. Whether you're passionate about entrepreneurship, philanthropy, or preserving a family business, your legacy plan should be as unique as your journey to success.

The question isn't whether these elements matter. How well does your current plan address them? Are you building a legacy that truly reflects what matters most to you and your family?

Conclusion

Everything we've explored in this chapter from the Anderson family's strategic gifting approach to the core elements of successful legacy planning points to one fundamental truth. Legacy is more than what you leave behind; it's what you set in motion today.

Whether you're structuring your business succession, creating lasting impact through charitable structures, or preparing the next generation through family education, taking action now shapes how your legacy unfolds.

Building a lasting legacy creates something meaningful that grows stronger with each passing generation.

Chapter 11

Your Path Forward

You've made it through this book, and, by now, you understand something most people never will. The tax code isn't your enemy. It's actually a powerful tool for building wealth, provided you know how to implement it correctly.

We've seen countless examples of both business owners and W-2 earners eliminating their tax burden legally and ethically. Are you ready to take action?

1. **Assess Your Current Situation**
    - Gather your recent tax returns
    - What was your tax liability in recent years?
    - Calculate your current tax burden

- Identify areas where you're leaving money on the table
- Review your existing entity structures (if any)

2. **Define Your Goals**

- Don't just focus on tax savings. Think bigger!
- What's your vision for wealth building?
- How do you want to protect your assets?
- What legacy do you want to create?
- Which tax incentives align with your business goals?

3. **Build Your Implementation Framework**

Remember the Four Circles:

- Tax Efficiency: with strategies involving entities, deductions, conversion, brackets, elimination, and deferral
- Specialization: Focus on strategies that match your situation and overlap with your interests
- Velocity: Plan for time-sensitive opportunities
- Leverage: Consider opportunities for strategic debt and collaborating with experts

4. **Create Your Documentation Wall**

Start building your audit protection now:

- Set up systems for tracking activities
- Organize your entity documentation
- Create clear separation between business and personal
- Maintain proper records from day one

I know it seems like a lot, but understand that you don't have to figure this out alone. In fact, trying to implement advanced tax strategies without proper guidance often leads to costly mistakes.

We're here to provide coordinated expertise that ensures proper implementation while protecting your wealth.

If you're ready to take the next step, I would love to help! But whether you choose to work with us or not, remember that the path to zero tax starts with a single decision. The decision to act. Don't wait until it's too late!

Resources and Social Media

Turn your phone's camera to the QR code below to access the links to reach out to us.

About The Author

From the fairways of professional golf to the complex terrain of tax strategy, Jeremy Lederer's journey reflects his life's mission. He aims to help successful entrepreneurs and W-2 professionals keep more of what they earn.

Watching his father navigate the challenges of business ownership, Jeremy witnessed firsthand how taxes often become the largest obstacle to growth and prosperity. This insight sparked a transformation that would lead him to revolutionize how high-performing individuals approach tax strategy.

Based between San Clemente, California, and Telluride, Colorado, Jeremy pioneered the Zero Tax Strategy for XIT CPA, a systematic approach that turns the tax code from a burden into a wealth-building tool.

Unlike traditional CPAs who focus solely on tax preparation, Jeremy recognizes that even brilliant strategies remain theoretical without proper execution. This realization led him to build a business so confident in its approach that it offers something unheard of in the tax industry. He provides a money-back guarantee if he and his team cannot create more value than their fees during the strategy development phase. He can proudly say that this guarantee has never been claimed.

Today, Jeremy leads XIT CPA, a sophisticated virtual family office, bringing together elite professionals across multiple disciplines to help clients legally eliminate their tax burden while building lasting wealth.

"Most people view the tax code as a burden," he often shares, "but it's actually a roadmap of incentives designed to reward specific behaviors that benefit the economy."

Through his innovative approach, unwavering commitment to implementation, and passion for education, Jeremy continues to show entrepreneurs and professionals across America that zero tax isn't just a dream. It's an achievable reality with the right strategy and execution.

www.ingramcontent.com/pod-product-compliance
Lightning Source LLC
LaVergne TN
LVHW022216200926
848481LV00006B/1996